Humanizing the Digital

Humanizing the Digital

Unproceedings from the MCN 2018 Conference

Edited by
Suse Anderson, Isabella Bruno, Hannah Hethmon,
Seema Rao, Ed Rodley, and Rachel Ropeik

AD HOC MUSEUM COLLECTIVE

To Adrienne, with love

Contents

Introduction

The Museum Computer Network (MCN) 2018 conference, "Humanizing the Digital", explored how museums can use digital technologies to foster human connection and dialogue, advance accessibility and inclusion, and champion inquiry and knowledge. Over the course of three days and more than one hundred and forty presentations, participants were barraged with examples of how the field continues to rely on the very human qualities of collaboration, creativity, and empathy to do our work, even in the digital work we do. If anything, "humanizing" seemed an even larger presence than "digital."

After witnessing the presentations, and taking part in some of the rich conversations that arose from them, a group of us came together to explore how best to capture and disseminate some of the learnings that occurred at the conference, to put some of that lightning in a bottle, as it were. The outcome of some intense conversations was a decision to ask the community to reflect on the conference and the ideas it sparked for them and to self-publish them. And given the speed at which our community moves and iterates, we decided it made sense to put the entire book (print and ebook) together in four months and have it ready for the Museums and Web conference in April, 2019. Since none of this would have happened without the conference, we decided to donate any profits to the MCN Scholarship fund.

What is this book? It is not a conference proceedings *per se*, and not a greatest hits collection. In fact, we were most interested in what happened *after* all the presentations were completed. What themes emerged in the hallways, how did people respond to what was going on around them? We thought it would be a worthwhile experiment to see if we could produce a book that reflected not *what went into* making the conference, which is what proceedings usually do, but to capture some of *what came out* of the conference; the learnings, the little epiphanies, the synthesizing that is rarely collected and preserved.

It is worth noting that we were midway through the process before it occurred to us that it might be a good idea to notify MCN that we were doing this. Thankfully, MCN thought that this kind of community-driven effort was worth embracing. Though unofficial, it is definitely aligned with MCN's mission of connecting people to ideas and each other. It is also a great example of the kind of community MCN has developed; one that is deeply collegial, true to its grassroots origins, geared toward action, and likely to ask for forgiveness before permission.

It is also worth noting that our editorial process followed (or, at least, tried to follow) those same principles. Editors and authors volunteered their time to this publication, which involved a social-media-based Call For Proposals that was open to anyone willing to put in the time and energy to turn something around within a matter of weeks. We did a bit of peer review for clarity, but relatively little editing of our submissions, so what you are about to read represents the varied voices and styles of the authors. While not every initial proposal ended up in this collection, we heartily thank all the members of the MCN community who shared their thoughts with us.

So that's how you hold this book, "Humanizing the Digital Museum" in your hand. It is necessarily a fragmentary reflection on a large event, but even in this small, kaleidoscopic view, we think you will find some of the energy and exciting thinking that was happening in Denver. And we look forward to seeing what you do with it to carry the work forward.

Ad Hoc Museum Collective Editorial Team,
Suse Anderson
Isabella Bruno
Hannah Hethmon
Seema Rao
Ed Rodley
Rachel Ropeik

Chapter 1

A Theme for Museum Technology

Chad Weinard

"Humanizing the Digital" marked a bit of a rhetorical about-face. For most of its short history, museum technology has been about "digitizing the human." Technologists endeavored to bring digital tools to bear on the mission of museums, in service of cultural heritage. At first that meant digitizing cultural collections, creating digital images and converting ledgers and card catalogues into databases. About 10 years ago, the process accelerated and gathered momentum, to include websites, social media, in-gallery interactives, and even museum processes and approaches. In the last two years, as the failings of digital culture have become shockingly apparent, we've seen a shift.

What if the most pressing problem today isn't the lack of digital tools in cultural heritage, but rather the lack of humanity in digital culture? Are museum technologists in a unique position to critique and change digital culture?

These were the questions running through my mind as notifications from the MCN program committee flooded my phone. I'd been reflecting on the impact of *Pink Art*, an exhibition that had recently closed at my museum, and deep in conversation with colleagues on the state of museum technology. When the program committee discussed ideas for a theme, I posted some quick thoughts on "Humanizing the Digital," and it stuck. Once it's official, a good conference theme means many things to many people; I'm grateful for the chance to think more about what it meant to me, and how it came to be.

For a mere tagline, the conference theme actually encompasses a fair bit of history, idealism gone astray, and newfound opportunity.

1.

For me, *Pink Art* suggested a new direction for museum technology. *Pink Art* was an exhibition I helped develop at the Williams College Museum of Art that explored WCMA's collection through the lens of color. From the start, the exhibition was a "digitizing humanity" project, by the end, it was clear that the lasting impact was in "humanizing the digital."

In order to look at fifteen thousand objects through "rose-colored glasses" (so to speak), we leveraged digital tools and approaches. We had a huge head start, thanks to all the labor that went into creating and keeping the digital images and records we required. (*Accession Number*, an earlier WCMA exhibition, shone a light on the history of WCMA's collection data, gathered from the first curator's leather-bound ledger, then painstakingly transcribed to index cards, to a database, and on to another database.) All that was a prelude to a recent digital initiative called *WCMA Digital* that was working to augment, package and share WCMA's collection data and images, making them available for research and creative use; this set the stage for *Pink Art*.

With data and images at the ready, how then do you rank a collection by "pinkness"? You start by defining the color "pink." It turns out everyone has a different idea of what pink is, and no one on the exhibition team—not the curators, not the exhibition designer, not interpretation or technologists—wanted to decide for everyone. And so, we crowdsourced the definition of "pink." A simple web app was developed that encouraged users to select the "pink" squares from a 4x4 grid of colors. Submit, select, repeat. The app provided a somewhat soothing, rather mindless, sometimes surprisingly social activity; in return, with each submission, the app was refining a model that defined "pink."

Now that we had a definition of "pink," we could rank the collection images. It turns out that defining what makes a painting "pink" is nearly as hard as defining the color "pink." Is it the picture whose digital image has the most pixels closest to "pink"? What about the painting whose small patch of "pink" nevertheless utterly defined the work of art? Was a tiny pink picture pinker than a giant picture with a fraction of pink? What about photographs that turn pink with age? Five computer science students crafted algorithms to give a "pink"-ness score to each collection image, and to show their work. The algorithms were as individual as the students:

"Islandize," for instance, preferred art with solid patches of pink; "Toon" started by transforming images to pictures akin to an animation cell (because the author loves anime); "Crayola" matched colors to one of eleven crayon "pinks." There was no right approach—each algorithm provided its own very idiosyncratic perspective on the collection.

Each object now had not one pinkness score, but five. We combined them, averaged them, created color-coded spreadsheets and visualizations. The algorithms provided opinionated new perspectives to consider. The curatorial team consulted each, crafted a final checklist, and developed an installation and interpretation plan.

So, was *Pink Art* "curated by algorithms?" This was an important question we heard often. The easy answer was no, and the larger lesson was that no exhibition could ever be. Even if the data and images going into the algorithms were pristine (they're textured and varied and incomplete), even if the algorithm was perfect and objective (like all algorithms, ours were handmade, full of human choices and biases), there would still need to be a human curator behind it all, caring for the data, directing the development of algorithms, deciding what to do with the output, arranging the works of art on the wall, and sharing the experience with the world.

While the exhibition offered a unique new perspective on the collection, connecting rarely-seen works to recent acquisitions through color, it was the algorithmic process that, for many, stole the show. The exhibition opened in the fall of 2017, at a time when media conversations about "fake news," the excesses of innovation culture, and the dangers of data and algorithms were ascendant. The prevailing narrative espoused by the technology industry—that data and algorithms are objective, mechanical, unbiased and unquestionable—was cracking.

In public programs for *Pink Art*, conversations focused on the nature of algorithms. Our students wrote algorithms that were quirky, opinionated, expressive, and full of personality. The exhibition and the art drew out these qualities and made them more apparent. It's plain to see that works of art can't be reduced to data and pixels; they are physical objects that embody myriad human choices, decisions, indecisions; they are fluid and impossible to quantify; they bring a mythology of objectivity and mechanical certainty to its knees—even the myth that surrounds the words "data" and "algorithm." Art helped us show that our data and algorithms were handmade, flawed, contingent, susceptible to bias, history, power; visitors learned the same is true for all algorithms. Further, the art objects also humanized the process of making. Working with art allowed the students to embrace the idea that making algorithms is a creative process, as much "creative writing" as "writing code." It's learning a language to express yourself in new ways.

We began the exhibition with a notion of showing off the power of digital tools to see the collection in new ways, and came out with important realizations of the imprint of humanity on digital processes and culture.

2.

Pink Art became part of an emerging conversation around "digital humanities" as well. Williams College is a premier liberal arts institution in which the arts are central; the art department has a prestigious history, and the art museum is a marquee public-facing institution known for innovative collaborations across campus. While there is no "digital humanities" program per se, there are faculty bringing digital tools and approaches to humanities research, and the art museum is well-positioned to connect the digital and the humanities through a project called *WCMA Digital*. The project enhances museum collection data, and encourages new digital approaches and tools. Indeed, the project even includes a Digital Humanities Postdoc Fellow to support faculty collaborations and projects. It makes perfect sense at Williams for the art museum to be the hub for innovation, collaboration and co-creation.

Bringing digital to the humanities was expected; the opportunity to bring the humanities to the digital was not. Enrollment in computer science classes has exploded at colleges and universities across the country, and there's a shortage of professors—new Ph.D.'s are joining industry instead of academia. The Computer Science department at Williams faces these challenges as well, but it also sees an opportunity. Many institutions of higher learning—especially large research universities—can supply industry with proficient coders. As critiques of digital culture are quick to point out, however, the failings of industry are rarely technical. What industry needs are skilled technologists with a broader background—a perspective on how their work affects people, a grounding in history, social science, moral philosophy and creative practice. Williams is uniquely-suited to graduate humanist technologists like this, that can build mindfully and affect change in a post-digital culture.

At Williams, the art museum helps develop humanist technologists. WCMA's collection data and image files provide a common language for interaction. It's important that intro students can work with data quickly and easily; even beginners can download a csv and a zip file of collection thumbnails and start exploring right away. Moreover, museum data wears its heart on its sleeve: it's quirky and textured, it reflects institutional history, it's actively maintained and changing. It's a great example of how data is subjective and contingent. Likewise, art images test the limits of taxonomy and analysis. *WCMA Digital* introduces students to the field of museum technology, and (with the Library and the IT department) to the notion of non-profit, non-commercial technology more broadly. Working with the museum expands the perception of coding as a creative process and personal practice, and code as an agent of change. The art museum provides a public interface for computer scientists to share ideas, to think through issues of usability and social impact.

3.

So does this paradigm shift from "digitizing humanity" to "humanizing digital"—the dynamic we saw in *Pink Art*, and in digital humanities on campus—have an analog in museum technology more broadly? Does it offer a chance to reflect on the past, and perhaps a path forward? This is the conversation I sought through MCN in 2018.

Ten years ago, museum technology was in an innovation phase, bringing an expanding array of new digital tools and approaches into the cultural sector. The web was mature and accessible, mobile was exploding, social media was transforming the landscape. Museum technologists weren't alone in their idealism: powerful digital tools, expanded networks, more-connected people would mean a better society. Museums needed to act fast, or face disruption or irrelevance; this was a common driver for innovation culture. Much needed to be built, and fast: new mobile websites with content management systems, online collections, exhibition microsites, mobile apps, new visitor info screens, touchscreen interactives, new social media accounts, email templates. The new work required new processes, new approaches, a new mindset for organizations.

This innovation phase was largely additive; it didn't fundamentally change the museum. Museum technologists benefitted from earlier work done in digitization and collections management; elaborate digital projects were built atop existing infrastructure without changing it or enhancing it. Indeed, in many cases the emerging "digital" positions in museums were separate from existing IT departments. This led to a "two-track I.T." approach, one fast and charged with innovation, the other slow and responsible for maintenance. As in the larger innovation culture, speed and agility came at the cost of sustainability and lasting change.

Now we see where innovation culture failed. Social media networks became weaponized, data breaches undermined trust, trackers monetized attention, creative tools shuttered or transformed due to shareholder pressure. Even in museum technology, the idealism has faded. Innovative digital labs have disbanded or restructured. The ambitious digital projects built a decade ago have been retired; their impact is hard to discern. Meanwhile the systems software that was ignored in the rush to innovation—the collections management systems, the membership software, the DAMS—remains. It hasn't changed at all from its pre-internet foundations. In some cases, platforms and approaches that were enlisted directly from industry now challenge museums' core values (Facebook, Google Analytics); others that were enlisted as infrastructure have effectively disappeared (Flickr).

In some ways, the "digital humanities" approach, bringing digital tools to bear on the preservation and presentation of cultural heritage collections, has been transformative. (Digitization, for instance, has laid a foundation for the future.) In other ways, it's not lived up to its promise.

What would it mean for the museum technology sector to embrace "humanizing the digital"? What would it look like for museums to offer an alternative to innovation culture and surveillance capitalism? How might museum technologists bring a humanities approach and values to bear on technology culture?

Here are a few ideas that came up in Denver, and percolated since:

1. **Look long-term**. Museums are charged with keeping objects forever; that gives museum technologists a unique and countercultural perspective. Museum technologists keep the objects' stories alive for generations to come. Systems and formats will change, but the living, growing, changing data around collection objects—the human context that give the objects meaning—needs care and oversight.

2. **Embrace maintenance**. If innovation culture is about disruption, creative destruction, "moving fast and breaking things," then maintenance culture (and museum culture) is about fixing, stewarding, sustaining. Perhaps ironically, maintenance encourages incremental improvement, and iterative, agile approaches.

3. **Innovate on infrastructures**. Innovation culture has given maintenance a bad name; infrastructure needs daring new ideas. Museum technologists are in a unique position to innovate on technology infrastructure, building sustainable core systems that make dynamic experiences easier to create and maintain. Technologists are already bringing new ideas to other museum infrastructures: processes, governance, org charts, staffing, strategy.

4. **Focus on values**. Technologies are not neutral. Each comes with a cost and values baked in. Museum technologists should strive to align technology decisions with museum values, and lead discussions around privacy, data stewardship, algorithmic bias, etc.

5. **Design for social impact**. Museum technologists work in public, in institutions that measure for public impact, in person and beyond. We have the opportunity to internalize institutional goals and build for good. Even internal museum tools and infrastructure can be designed for positive impact among staff.

How can a museum technologist change the world? There are precious few opportunities in the job market for creative technologists to work for good; the technology industry puts most to work in the service of surveillance capitalism. In museums (as in higher education, and libraries), technologists can build with an eye toward social good, sustainability, and long-term impact.

We face monumental challenges, and thoughtfully reorienting our relationship to technology is one. Is there a place for museums in finding solutions? Can museum technologists lead the way?

Chapter 2

Calm Technology in Museums

Cathy Sigmond

Introduction

What is Calm Technology? How do the principles of Calm Technology apply to museums?

In her keynote address at the Museum Computer Network (MCN) 2018 conference in Denver, Colorado, user experience designer and cyborg anthropologist Amber Case discussed Calm Technology,[1] which she described as a design philosophy that aims to respect our "humanness" by reducing complexity to promote focus and calm.[2] She outlined the underlying principles of Calm Technology, which she claims work together to "conserve and respect human attention."[3] While Case's keynote address did not focus on museums specifically, her ideas resonated with me as a museum evaluator. My work in evaluation centers on helping museum professionals better understand how the products they create—whether a program, an exhibition, piece of technology, or anything else—are "working" for visitors. Conserving and respecting people's attention is both fundamental and crucial to designing something that "works."

In this essay, I draw on Case's keynote address and explore how we might apply the principles of Calm Technology to our work in museums, and in what ways, if any, the principles of Calm Technology can help us design museum experiences so they best serve visitors.

Calm Technology in Brief

The phrase "Calm Technology" was first coined in the 1990s by researchers studying human-computer interaction at Xerox's Palo Alto Research Center (Xerox PARC). Three of these researchers, Mark Weiser, John Seely Brown, and Rich Gold, believed that technology was becoming increasingly complex and thus placing competing demands on our attention. Their chief concern was that a future saturated with devices and connected networks would have a negative impact on human behavior and our general well-being.[4] In her MCN keynote, Case argued that this idea was far ahead of its time—the researchers at Xerox PARC were able to foresee many of the threats that poorly-designed technology would pose to our well-being, long before smartphones and the internet were ubiquitous.[5] Weiser, Brown, and Gold envisioned a future where technology disappeared into the background, allowing us to go about our lives assisted by—but not distracted by—technology. Weiser sums it up well in this quotation:

> The most profound technologies are those that disappear. They weave themselves into the fabric of everyday life and are indistinguishable from it.[6]

One way to think about Calm Technology is simply as "non-intrusive" design.[7] The overarching goal is to design interactions—whether with a product or service, physical or digital—that are elegant and humane. Case argues that designing technology to be "calm" both respects our limited time and helps ease our cognitive load. That is, if good design allows someone to get to their goal with the *fewest steps*, designing something to be calm allows someone to get there with the *lowest mental cost*."[8] This is an important consideration because while the capabilities of machines have (and will continue to) rapidly improve, the limits of human cognition remain the same. Technology, therefore, should work *with* people and not *against* them.

Applying the Principles of Calm Technology to Museums

Case developed eight principles for designing Calm Technology that expand on the Xerox PARC researchers' original ideas. These principles are important for anyone designing new technologies in today's hyper-connected and smart device-filled world to keep in mind, but I also see them as incredibly useful for thinking through designing museum experiences, and more specifically, exhibitions. In the sections that follow, I discuss each of the eight principles of Calm Technology in the context of museums. My intention is to reiterate Case's ideas so as not to forget her intellectual labor, but also to expand on them and consider how they apply to the practical realities of designing for museums.

However, before going any further—one important caveat about the word "technology." In this essay (and in Case's and the Xerox PARC researchers' work), technology does not necessarily mean something "digital;" it simply means anything we design and build to help us accomplish a goal. Defined this way, technology encompasses everything from a tea kettle to a smoke alarm to an app.[9] Whether or not you agree with this broad definition, it is useful for helping us to recall an important point—that ultimately, we design things to be an extension of ourselves. In this way, technology is fundamentally human, no matter what form it takes.[10] This is an especially salient point when thinking about museums—institutions rooted in human stories and creativity—where the overarching goal of our work is always to make a positive impact on audiences.

Principle I: Technology should require the smallest possible amount of attention.

This idea is best summarized as follows: avoid information overload! In other words, technology should allow us to quickly surmise a crucial piece of information at a glance, without demanding our full attention. Case gives the example of the light on an oven that indicates whether it is preheated; you can quickly see if the oven is preheated based on whether or not the light is illuminated. This is also indicated by sound; an oven beeps when preheated, allowing the user to walk away while it heats up rather than wait and watch for the light to turn on.

The core component of this principle is its focus on our attention as a limited commodity. Attention, Case claims, is still not a widespread consideration when designing technologies. Arguably, the same is often true in museums. For instance, think about how many exhibitions still include copious amounts of text or long films, despite decades of timing and tracking studies that indicate the average length of time visitors spend in an *entire exhibition* is under 10 minutes.[11] While providing opportunities for deeper engagement is important, we should ensure that core information—the key takeaway—is always available to visitors at a glance. This applies whether the designed experience is a paper map of the museum, a single exhibit label, an interactive, an app, or an entire exhibition.

Principle II: Technology should inform and create calm.

This is the idea that technology can create a sense of calm by letting you know that a system is functioning correctly and that all is well, without demanding your full attention or creating friction. For instance, a tea kettle can be ignored most of the time, until it sings. It does not draw attention to itself until necessary. Another good example is anti-virus software, which continuously runs in the background on your computer and alerts you only when it has found something suspicious. The calm comes from knowing that you will be alerted at the appropriate time if something needs to be addressed.[12]

This idea overlaps with Principle I, but it emphasizes the *affective* response a designed experience should ideally instill in users. Applied to museums, this is another a reminder not to overwhelm visitors with information or instructions and to instead find ways for them to retain the sense of calm they (hopefully) walked in with. Doing so sets the stage for visitors to experience wonder and delight (two things you are unlikely to experience when overwhelmed). And, it leaves room for visitors to focus on enjoying time spent with family and friends instead of complex problem-solving.

Principle III: Technology should make use of the periphery.

A Calm Technology "moves easily from the periphery of our attention, to the center, and back;" and, the information in the periphery is informative without demanding our full focus.[13] The classic examples, according to Case, come from the experience of driving. When driving, our primary task is to pay attention to the road; however, using touch, sound, and peripheral vision can alert drivers of new information and allow them to complete secondary, supporting tasks while staying focused on the road. For instance, pushing on a handle to turn on your turn signal does not require you take your eyes off of the road, nor does turning on your high-beam headlights.

What I love about this principle is the inherent challenge to create experiences that minimize unnecessary distractions which reduce our ability to successfully accomplish a goal. In museums, consider the "goal" to be, for example, learning a key idea the exhibition intends to communicate, experiencing a particular emotion it intends to instill, or participating in an experience with others. When our attention is interrupted for something that is not crucial to supporting the goal, it ultimately makes it less likely that goal will be achieved. This principle begs the question of how we might better support visitors in achieving core intended outcomes by designing peripheral (secondary and tertiary) experiences more intentionally. For instance, how might 'attract screens' on interactives or films passively instill an intended emotion or inform visitors of a key message at a glance, in the event a visitor quickly walks by and never ends up stopping to use those exhibits in-depth?

Principle IV: Technology should amplify the best of technology and the best of humanity.

Put simply, this is the idea that machines should not act like humans and humans should not act like machines. Being human means seeking food and fun; being creative and caring about others; seeking social connections; and desiring meaning and belonging.[14] Humans are also uniquely capable of understanding context and abstraction, but machines cannot do this unless we teach them to; even then, there is a limit to their capabilities. The best technologies celebrate and *amplify* these qualities that make us human. This, Case argues, is what makes the Google search engine such great technology. Its core function is to connect us to all of the knowledge that other humans have created over time, fulfilling our natural desire for connection and belonging.

There are a few lessons for museums inherent in this principle. One is to be forgiving of the humanness of visitors when they have trouble using your designs. That is, respect people by providing support (both instructional and emotional) when human error inevitably occurs. This might even mean testing your designs to learn unexpected ways people use your creations and then redesigning *for* those tendencies rather than against them. It also means understanding that visitors will make connections between their personal experiences and the information/stories you provide that you never anticipated, and designing for and encouraging this behavior. In other words, we must design museum experiences that provide a variety of entry points for visitors to make connections. And, consider Case's example of the Google search engine as a technology that successfully amplifies the best of technology and the best of humanity. What parallels exist with museums' collections? What types of experiences might we create with our collections if we think about tools like our collections databases as avenues for human connection and socialization, rather than encyclopedic repositories?

Principle V: Technology can communicate, but it doesn't need to speak.

Here Case challenges us to think critically about whether words are really essential to effective and accessible communication. Does technology need to rely on voice, or can it use a different communication method? She gives the example of Roomba™, the popular hands-free robot vacuum. Roomba is universally understood because it communicates through sound and tone rather than through voice. When Roomba completes a task, it chirps; when it gets stuck, it emits a somber tone. Everyone understands this no matter their age or what language they speak.[15]

It is worth considering how museums might rely less on words in exhibitions to promote clarity and accessibility. The obvious tension here is that, as storytelling institutions, museums need to rely to some degree on words and voice to communicate stories. The question then becomes this: once we have pared down the words/voice to communicate only what is essential (recall Principles I and II), how do we leverage other communication methods to enhance the information communicated through words? Wayfinding is one obvious example of how museums often (though not always) successfully apply this idea; physical cues such as the placement of partitions, the size of openings, the intensity of lighting all suggest how visitors should move through a space. Are there other instances where nonverbal cues such as positive or negative tones, symbols, lights, or haptic features could successfully replace text or voice in an exhibition?

Principle VI: Technology should work even when it fails.

How, you might wonder, does something still work if it has failed? The answer is by building "edge cases"—scenarios that are unlikely to occur but that could occur—into the design. Case gives the example of an escalator, which reverts to a set of stairs if it stops moving, still allowing transportation from one floor of a building to another. Case argues that designers often ignore edge cases and instead design things that fail completely if one part of the design does not work as intended. This does not have to be a drastic, complete failure; only a small thing has to go wrong to make you lose focus or direction when trying to complete a task or achieve a goal. The key to avoiding derailment from the task at hand is to design systems that have a "fallback mode" that offers less functionality but still offers access to the basics.[16]

This mindset of flexibility and contingency planning is important for museums to adopt when designing for exhibitions. Put another way, how might we design exhibit experiences to account for things breaking? Or for small (yet impactful) distractions? If one feature of an exhibit breaks or is for some reason temporarily inaccessible, there needs to still be a way for visitors to interact with it and walk away with the big idea. Another way to think about potential "failure" in a museum setting is to consider that visitors are almost never alone when visiting an exhibition. More often than not, there are many potential distractions surrounding visitors (e.g., their phones, other visitors) that may keep them from achieving the museum's intended outcomes. The key to ensuring that visitors still achieve these outcomes is building in redundancy so that visitors can still walk away with the exhibition's big idea, even if they missed part of an exhibit because they were temporarily distracted.

Principle VII: The right amount of technology is the minimum needed to solve the problem.

This is essentially a call for simplicity. In other words, do not provide a user with more information or features than they need to accomplish a goal, or you risk confusing them and diluting their ability to accomplish the task you designed a tool or service to help them accomplish in the first place. It all comes down to alignment. Case poses the following question: "For each new feature, ask yourself, *is this something necessary to the product? Not fun, but necessary.* If it doesn't solve a core problem, don't build it." [17] [emphasis hers]

Of course, designing something simple is never a simple process. It usually requires months of planning, testing, and retesting to arrive at the simplest solution to accomplish your goals. Applied to museums, this is a call to both resist the urge to share every interesting fact or story (which would be overwhelming) and also to rigorously and continuously test your designs with actual visitors. If we don't keep this idea in mind when we design for exhibitions, we risk diluting the big ideas we hope to convey and the feelings we hope to instill in visitors. It helps to reframe Case's question using museum language: For each possible new piece of information or design feature, ask yourself, is this something *necessary to convey the key message? Not fun, but necessary.* If it doesn't reinforce the key message, don't say it.

Principle VIII: Technology should respect social norms.

The final principle asks us to take social context into consideration when designing something new. Technology (or a service) is readily accepted when it is perceived as "restoring" people back to a situation that's considered "normal." This, Case argues, is why eyeglasses and crutches are not fear-inducing pieces of technology. They give people capabilities that put them back in line with the expected state of seeing clearly and moving around. [18] It's when a technology is perceived to enhance or elevate our capabilities beyond what we are already used to that it risks becomes anxiety-inducing. Thus, it is important to *gradually* expand people's understandings of what is normal or acceptable by slowly—very slowly—introducing new features and concepts, one at a time, and allowing people to slowly adjust to the idea as it becomes the norm. [19]

Thinking again about museums, this is yet another call not to overwhelm visitors with a too many new experiences at once. If someone is not used to using a particular technology (e.g., augmented reality, virtual reality) at home, then they are unlikely to readily do so in the museum without any anxiety. To be clear, adhering to this principle does *not* mean avoiding taking risks or trying new things. It simply means slowly introducing those new things to visitors in a thought-out and coordinated way, rather than trying all the new things at once hoping to wow people. People need time to adjust to new circumstances.

Conclusion

Chances are that many of these ideas feel familiar, even if you've never heard of Calm Technology before reading this essay. That is because, although it arose from the field of human-computer interaction, it has a lot in common with other ways of thinking that we already draw inspiration from or use directly in the museum field. Consider human-centered design, user experience design, and intentional practice. All of these areas of practice focus on creating products and services that "work for people." Human-centered design is a framework that considers the human perspective throughout the design process, and can be applied to any discipline.[20] User experience design similarly considers all aspects of an end-user's interaction with a company, its services, and its products.[21] And in a broader vein that is more specific to museums, intentional practice asks museums to articulate the kind of impact they hope to achieve among audiences and align their actions accordingly.[22] All three of these frameworks place audiences at the center of our work.

Calm Technology offers a slightly different, but equally useful lens through which to view our work in museums. The principles of Calm Technology are simple, but it is often the simplest ideas that can have the greatest impact. Taken individually, each principle offers a useful constraint that can help weed out the aspects of a design that are not helping you or your visitors achieve a goal. All together, they are a set of values that all museum professionals should consider to inform a holistic approach to decision-making when working to create powerful and meaningful experiences—"technological" or otherwise—for visitors.[23]

NOTES

1. The phrase "Calm Technology" is capitalized here and throughout this essay to be consistent with Case's writings both online and in her book. Amber Case, *Calm Technology: Principles and Patterns for Non-Intrusive Design* (Sebastopol: O'Reilly Media, Inc., 2016), 15.

2. Amber Case, "About," *Case Organic,* https://caseorganic.com/about (accessed February 10, 2019)

3. Case, *Calm Technology,* 15.

4. Weiser and Brown published a series of research papers outlining the need for Calm Technology in the mid-1990s. They include the following and can all be accessed on Amber Case's website, https://calmtech.com/papers.html : Mark Weiser, "The Computer for the 21st Century," (September 1991); Mark Weiser and John Seely Brown, "Designing Calm Technology," (December 1995); and Mark Weiser and John Seely Brown, "The Coming Age of Calm Technology," (October 1996).

5. To draw attention to their work, Case wrote the book *Calm Technology,* where she reiterates Weiser, Brown, and Gold's ideas and expands on them to account for the passage of time

since their conception.

6. Weiser, "The Computer for the 21st Century," quoted in Case, *Calm Technology*, 15.

7. Case, *Calm Technology*, viii (preface).

8. Case, *Calm Technology*, 16.

9. Those who attended Case's keynote address at MCN 2018 might recall that she cited a tea kettle as an example of Calm Technology.

10. Case, *Calm Technology*, x (preface).

11. For a broad comparison of summative evaluation studies in museums, see: Beverly Serrell, *Paying Attention: Visitors and Museum Exhibitions* (Washington, D.C.: American Alliance Of Museums, 1998). This book that was first published in 1998 and that was supported by a National Science Foundation (NSF) grant called "A Meta-analysis of Visitor Time/Use in Museum Exhibitions." For an update from Serrell since the book was first published and a list of many other resources on timing and tracking studies, see: Beverly Serrell, "Field Trips Are Valuable Learning Experiences," *Informal Science*, July 8, 2016 http://www.informalscience.org/ news-views/paying-more-attention-paying-attention (accessed February 09, 2019). For a list of specific summative evaluation studies that including the timing and tracking methodology, see *Informal Science*, http://informalscience.org/search- results?search_api_views_fulltext=timing%20and%20tracking&f[1]=search_api_combined_2:41 (accessed February 10, 2019).

12. Case, *Calm Technology*, 20.

13. Amber Case, "Principles of Calm Technology," *Calm Tech*, https://calmtech.com/index.html (accessed February 10, 2019).

14. Case, *Calm Technology*, 29.

15. "Principles of Calm Technology."

16. Case, *Calm Technology*, 40.

17. Case, *Calm Technology*, 43.

18. Case, *Calm Technology*, 46.

19. Case, *Calm Technology*, 48.

20. Francesca Elisia, "What's the Difference Between Human-Centered Design and User Experience Design?," *Medium*, https://blog.prototypr.io/whats-the-difference-between- human-centred-design-and-user-experience-design-2f48e5c9be25 (accessed February 7, 2019).

21. Don Norman and Jakob Nielsen, "The Definition of User Experience (UX)," *Nielson Norman Group*, https://www.nngroup.com/articles/definition-user-experience/ (accessed February 7, 2019).

22. Randi Korn, *"Intentional Practice for Museums,"* (Lanham: Rowman & Littlefield, 2018), xix (preface).

23. Case, *Calm Technology,* 51.

BIBLIOGRAPHY

Case, Amber. "Calm Technology Papers." *Calm Tech.* https://calmtech.com/papers.html (accessed February 10, 2019).

Case, Amber. *Calm Technology: Principles and Patterns for Non-Intrusive Design.* Sebastopol: O'Reilly Media, Inc., 2016.

Case, Amber. "About." *Case Organic.* https://caseorganic.com/about/ (accessed February 10, 2019).

Elisia, Francesca. "What's the Difference Between Human-Centered Design and User Experience Design?." *Medium.* August 20, 2017. https://bit.ly/2CJK5P9 (accessed February 10, 2019).

Korn, Randi. *Intentional Practice for Museums.* Lanham: Rowman & Littlefield, 2018.

Norman, Don, and Jakob Nielson. "The Definition of User Experience (UX)." *Nielson Norman Group.* https://www.nngroup.com/articles/definition-user-experience/ (accessed February 7, 2019).

Serrell, Beverly. "Field Trips Are Valuable Learning Experiences." *Informal Science.* July 8, 2016. http://www.informalscience.org/news-views/paying-more-attention-paying-attention (accessed February 09, 2019).

Serrell, Beverly. *Paying Attention: Visitors and Museum Exhibitions.* Washington, D.C.: American Association of Museums, 1998.

Weiser, Mark, and John Seely Brown. "Designing Calm Technology." *Calm Technology Papers.* https://calmtech.com/papers/computer-for-the-21st-century.html (accessed February 10, 2019).

Weiser, Mark, and John Seely Brown. "The Coming Age of Calm Technology." *Calm Technology Papers.* https://calmtech.com/papers/coming-age-calm-technology.html (accessed February 10, 2019).

Weiser, Mark. "The Computer for the 21st Century." *Calm Technology Papers.* https://calmtech.com/papers/computer-for-the-21st-century.html (accessed February 10, 2019).

Chapter 3

Reimagining Social Influencers through an Invitation Culture

Lori Byrd-McDevitt

Every day opportunistic social influencers come knocking on our museum doors with requests that leave us bewildered, even as 40% of millennials are considering "instagrammability" when deciding their next travel destination. Museums are increasingly expected to compete with big, corporate brands on digital platforms while managing significantly fewer resources. But in an oversaturated market, museums are lucky to have the heart that many big brands lack. We can cultivate social influencers into communities who provide authentic connections to those audiences we have not been able to reach. Truly connecting with social influencers means embracing an invitation culture—building relationships, sharing experiences, and bringing the long-term, human connection back into our museums.

What is an invitation culture? The term may be most prevalent within the context of Protestant churches, encouraging congregations to invite new members to join their communities.[1] More recently, it has extended well beyond this scope to encompass underserved communities more generally. The premise is based simply on the notion of outreach. Invitation culture is the practice of inviting someone to join in when they would not have considered it themselves, or even would have felt actively prohibited from participating. A simple invitation can be incredibly uplifting and empowering for the individual who has until then felt unseen or undervalued.

At The Children's Museum of Indianapolis, we have built on the idea of invitation culture within our social influencer program since its inception in 2013. As the world's largest children's museum averaging over a million visitors annually, we are a natural draw for influencers and tourist writers in our region. We knew that establishing a strong network of influencers would help us connect to the local community and, by extension, build the museum's brand. No matter the museum's size, influencers matter. Every museum has something to give, and there is an influencer out there that loves your mission and wants to share it.

Over time, our existing group of influencers at The Children's Museum began to recommend others with like-minded interests who we may have overlooked. This caused our community to exponentially grow into a network of loyal ambassadors for the museum. We now have relationships with around fifty core influencers who consistently attend events. These fifty are among 130 local and regional influencers who remain actively on our list. Over seven years, due to the niche interests of specific exhibits, we have been in touch with over 200 total influencers, and our list is ever-growing.

A key way to invite influencers to connect with you is to host events. The Children's Museum's exhibit preview parties have occurred for over five years, and have become a tradition in the community. The previews are more than an exclusive sneak peek to an exhibit, they are our way to invite influencers in, to show them we value their support, and to make them feel a part of the museum family. They are also an opportunity for attendees to network and build partnerships with one another. The events are focused on ensuring attendees have a great time—providing food, giveaways, social screens, and low expectations for promotional coverage. The social media comes authentically and organically, while building something even more important—loyalty and trust.

When doing all of this inviting, how do you know when someone is truly a "social influencer?" When documentarian Asri Bendacha traveled the world to speak to social influencers about their rise to fame, many did not feel comfortable calling themselves "influencers." Rather, they felt this distinction should come from the collaborator.[2] The definition is also not about follower number. What's more important is audience and brand relevance, which will be specific to your museum. In the marketing field a capital "I" "Influencer" is an Instagrammer with millions of followers, like celebrities.[3] More recently, "micro-influencers" have become commonplace in marketing collaborations with many brands. Micro-influencers are defined as accounts with tens to hundreds of thousands of followers. Now the "nanoinfluencers," those with as few as a thousand followers, are the trend.[4]

A nanoinfluencer—any social media user with an engaged following, no matter the follower count—is beneficial for a museum. In an era when online users are tiring of subliminal influencer advertising, authenticity is crucial. Museums have experience-based content that influencers will enthusiastically share to break through the monotony. Instagrammers with fewer followers are often eager to collaborate and efficiently share your message while expecting less from you. A museum's true community, who is more likely to care for your museum and its mission, can be found in these nanoinfluencers. Sometimes, implementing an invitation culture means inviting someone to be an influencer when they did not even realize they could be one. Imagine the joy you can instill by messaging an unsuspecting social media user to tell them their social account is valuable to your museum and you want to invite them to join in exclusive opportunities? You have officially secured a loyal influencer for years to come.

We've learned at The Children's Museum that social influencer strategy should not stop at the social media manager's desk. If the corner-office is discussing partner or donor buy-in on a project, they should be talking about influencer buy-in, too. Influencer support is extremely important due to how fast they can spread the word online, or be your eyes and ears in the private back-channels of the internet. For us, what started as invitations to participate in collaborative events grew into personal relationships with our team, and over the years, even friendships. This came out of the mutual trust built by maintaining the key understanding that the influencer email list would not be used for promotional purposes. Now our influencers are proactively loyal and willing to help whenever needed. For instance, our team can send a quick Direct Message to a couple of friends to get some honest feedback on a campaign. Frequently, influencers will tag us in local Facebook groups when questions or concerns arise before a situation gets out of control.

Do not underestimate the power of a successful long-term influencer relationship. The Children's Museum has repeatedly called upon key influencers to share about major announcements at important times. One example is when local blogger, "The Queen of Free," used her column on the city tourism website to announce our complicated admission change to Dynamic Pricing to illustrate her buy-in on a change that could have had a negative reaction. This was an example of a long-time relationship coming to our assistance at a decisive moment. At The Children's Museum, over the years ultimately we gave a little, but we received a lot.

When you take the time to put your heart into a social influencer strategy, the result can be at its foundation a mutually beneficial bridge to your community, and at its best a long-term friendship with a loyal group of online ambassadors. So tap into that thing that makes your museum win at "instagrammability"—that unique experience, the fun, the learning, the inspiration. By embracing a culture of invitation, we can allow social media influencers to bring an authentic human connection back into our museums.

NOTES

1. Jim Burnett, "Creating a Culture of Invitation," *Facts and Trends*, LifeWay, April 6, 2017, https://factsandtrends.net/2017/04/06/creating-a-culture-of-invitation (accessed February 9, 2019).

2. Asri Bendancha, dir, *Follow Me*, (Singapore: Netflix Productions, 2018) https://www.netflix.com/title/81037898

3. Brett Farmiloe, "The Power of Micro-Influencers on Instagram," *SocialMediaToday*, Industry Dive, August 23, 2018, https://www.socialmediatoday.com/news/the-power-of-micro-influencers-on-instagram/530743/ (accessed Feburary 10, 2019).

4. Sapna Maheshwari, "Are You Ready for the Nanoinfluencers?," *The New York Times*, November 11, 2018, https://www.nytimes.com/2018/11/11/business/media/nanoinfluencers-instagram-influencers.html (accessed February 10, 2019).

BIBLIOGRAPHY

Asri Bendancha, dir. *Follow Me*. Singapore: Netflix Productions, 2018. https://www.netflix.com/title/81037898

Burnett, Jim. "Creating a Culture of Invitation." *Facts and Trends*. LifeWay, April 6, 2017. https://factsandtrends.net/2017/04/06/creating-a-culture-of-invitation/ (accessed January 18, 2019).

Farmiloe, Brett. "The Power of Micro-Influencers on Instagram." *SocialMediaToday*. IndustryDive, August 23, 2018. http://www.socialmediatoday.com/news/the-power-of-micro-influencers-on-instagram/530743/ (accessed January 18, 2019).

Maheshwari, Sapna. "Are You Ready for the Nanoinfluencers?" *The New York Times*, November 11, 2018. http://www.nytimes.com/2018/11/11/business/media/nanoinfluencers-instagram-influencers.html (accessed January 18, 2019).

Wilson, Mitzi. "How Influencers are Turning the Business of Travel on Its Head." *Social Pro Daily*. Adweek, May 11, 2018. http://www.adweek.com/digital/how-influencers-are-turning-the-business-of-travel-on-its-head (accessed January 18, 2019).

Chapter 4

Humanizing the Video: A Reflection on MCN's Media Production Process

Andrew Mandinach

Capturing the Spirit of MCN

For me, MCN is like a winter camp for cultural organizations. We convene annually, usually reuniting with the same faces year after year. Instead of campfires we gather around Ignite speeches, and we close out in song during karaoke. Our sessions are complemented by a plethora of additional activities including city tours and receptions. And best of all, many people form bonds that extend beyond the conference, corresponding throughout the year, both professionally and personally. While my comparison of MCN to a winter camp may come off as a lighthearted dismissal of what MCN's organizers set out to do, it's actually meant to encompass the broader impact that MCN has on people's lives. To simply call it a conference doesn't begin to describe what one takes away from MCN beyond technical training. Whether you're a long-returning attendee or a newcomer eager to network there's a place for you to learn, to share, and to lead. Look no further than the Ignite presentations, a high-energy series of talks where the audience support is as significant as the speaking. I don't doubt that the name Ignite was chosen for a reason. A palpable energy is created that first night that runs throughout the course of the conference. I'd even go as far to say, it runs throughout the entire organization and makes it so easy to become involved with the MCN community. At least that's how it happened for me.

For the past three years, I served as the conference media production chair, and it's been my goal to try and capture the spirit of each conference and present it during the closing plenary's end of conference highlight video. The highlight videos have become the vehicle for which we're able to reflect on what's been said and done by a wide range of attendees, over the course of four days, including our scholars, sponsors, mentors and mentees, and attendees of various disciplines and seniority. It's a reflection of who we are and what we're talking about as an organization.

I joined the media production team in 2015 and assisted in the production of the first highlight video for MCN. The directive of Anna Chiaretta Lavatelli, chairperson at that time, was to produce something that didn't just feature conference veterans or board members, but to share experiences of folks who were like me: new and excited to learn and become involved. It's easy enough to have leadership tell you how things are meant to be felt. It's another to get folks to talk specifically about what excites them, what they've learned, and what new strategies and tactics they'll return to their workplace with. Since then, I've probably produced over 100 interviews, listening to each conference and editing the takeaways. And I would say there's been a change in the conversations taking place at MCN. Not only in what we're talking about, but how it's been recorded. We have gone from learning how to use our tools, to learning how to use them well, and for the benefit of others.

A History of Responding to the Needs of the MCN Community

Creating content for the benefit of the community has become the core consideration guiding the discussion on how to document the conference. And while it's become one of the most engaging videos produced, the highlight video is only part of a much larger effort in documentation. The methods have changed, but the efforts to document have largely consisted of recording all sessions, as well as the Ignite talks, the keynote lecture and keynote in conversation; not to mention the pre-conference big idea videos. The highlight video captures the experience of the conference, and the rest serve as archival resources for the community. I think it's worth making the distinction between the two because the highlight videos serve a very specific purpose, different than the rest of the documentation for the conference. See, it takes a lot to actually do what we do—not just capturing everything, but editing it all, and doing so in a timely manner. Our current consideration is about producing content that can be used as tools beyond the conference, but the earliest discussions were about how to document. The first MCN videos from 2011, recorded by conference volunteers, were mainly room recordings of presentations. Then in 2013, Anna started to hire & direct local videographers in order to increase bandwidth and quality. This was the first shift in our process and purpose from documentation to production, from archive to sharable resource. By 2015 our hired teams were recording every presentation from sessions to Ignites, with conference volunteers, myself included, assisting in assembling edits, organizing the massive increase in media files, and determining what a newly produced highlight video should feel like. Yet despite being able to record all sessions, viewership did follow the same upward trajectory. As a result, in 2016 all sessions were audio recorded and then transcribed to make our files more accessible, and by extension searchable. We attempted to shift from sharable resource to searchable tool.

This history highlights how our process to document the conference goes beyond just creating an archive of information. The evolving considerations that I have weighed for the past three years, same as Anna before me, and now Kathryn Quigley after me, reflect the evolving nature of our industry. Video producers throughout the field are asking the same questions. How do we tell the stories of our organizations through the voices of those organizations? Our challenges to document the conference demonstrate the fact that humanizing our digital projects isn't something that happens overnight. It is a long process that takes time to implement, test, and adapt to responses. The question is no longer about our capability to do so. In 2017, I facilitated the hiring of a full-time MCN videography team. Until this point the hired teams turned over each year, and it was the job of MCN video volunteers to ensure that MCN's voice was not lost in the newly formalized documentation process. This new-found permanence has allowed us to build upon our work and rather than reinvent the wheel each year. While preserving and archiving our conference is important, recording conference sessions has proven to not be as useful a tool as we imagined—at least not in the way we've been producing them. If viewership isn't there, it begs the question: do we keep recording sessions like we've been doing? For me the answer is connected to the shift in the conversations we're hearing, a shift from professional development to what I think can be called professional wellness.

Moving from Professional Development to Professional Wellness

This idea of collective wellness stems from a quote that Tim Svenonius makes in the 2015 highlight video. He says "we're giving ourselves, we're giving one another, permission to talk about some things that are just not discussed that much in museum communities."[1] Referring to the political/global "undercurrents" as Seema Rao appropriately goes on to describe them, Tim literally signaled how social change had inextricably become part of MCN's conversations. Or at least he did so on record for the first time. Initially we gave ourselves permission to have the conversations between sessions. And I would say we continue to do so through sessions following Chatham House Rule. A year after Tim's remark, Chatham House Rule started to impact our production workflow. For the first time the discussion became about *not* recording a session. "When a meeting, or part thereof, is held under the Chatham House Rule, participants are free to use the information received, but neither the identity nor the affiliation of the speaker(s), nor that of any other participant, may be revealed."[2] What started as being asked to not record a session or two, has become an official format for session proposals, taken on by the organization. The increase in sessions following Chatham House Rule and other alternative presentation styles demonstrate a growing desire among attendees to sharing more openly and authentically with each other. Sessions across the board have moved from case studies demonstrating how org 'X' caught lightning in a bottle, to providing toolkits that enabled attendees to capture their own lightning in a bottle.

If people come to MCN for the professional development, they stay for the support. I guess that can be said of any organization, but to talk about what we learn at MCN is to talk about the community we learn it with. A good example of this is illustrated in the un-conference open mic sessions that took place on the last day of this year's conference. The session I attended started with a simple question written on an easel pad: "what are you reading?" Facilitated by Seema Rao and Adrienne Lalli Hills, the discussion evolved from compiling a list of professional reading materials, to addressing the ways and reasons people publish—or don't - their scholarship.[3] This session and the broader decision to program an un-conference open-mic demonstrates how MCN empowers attendees to check in with others. We recharge as we exchange ideas, work through institutional roadblocks, and push the limits of our own capabilities.

These types of sessions are cathartic, they're supportive, and they're imbued with self-care. And when I refer to self, I refer to a collective self of a community working to heal its members. An example of this, and one that followed Chatham House Rule was the session, 'The In-Between: How to Facilitate Interdepartmental Collaboration from the Institutional Middle.' Carissa Dougherty, Amanda Dearolph, Ellice Engdahl, Lisel Record, Mark McKay, and Victoria Portway started by introducing themselves and identified six types of management/team communication scenarios experienced by people in an "in between" position. After defining an in-between position as, "a position where you take on the role of translator, liaison, and/or cheerleader to break down silos and foster digital literacy among coworkers," attendees self-selected a group to join and discuss.[4] The only issue with this session was that too many people identified with too many of the topics the various groups were discussing. It's important to note that this was officially listed on the MCN website as a "workshop-roundtable-therapy-session." This wasn't a formal presentation on communication best-practices in complicated workplaces. It was a discussion amongst colleagues to provide different perspectives for various scenarios examining the nuances of interdepartmental collaboration. People were able to share genuine concerns and frustrations. They were heard and recognized. Take that and follow it up with Susan Edwards, Michelle Grohe, and Kathryn Quigley's session, "Talk to Your Visitors: DIY Human-Centered Research" and you've got yourself quite the self-empowering day.[5] Okay, they were on two different days, but you get the point. Their three case studies demonstrated how human-centered design could be used as a way to connect with visitors. And demonstrate they did. Participants engaged in active listening exercises and conducted empathy interviews in the room for the purpose taking feedback home, not just instructions.

Video as a Mirror of the Organization

This year's theme follows a long history of working to advance the field by focusing on empowering the people who utilize the tools of the trade, rather than the tools themselves. Before attending my first MCN in 2014, I thought session tracks would be segregated by field of interest: the social media kids in one room; the video kids in another; the educators in another. While it's not to say that doesn't occur, what I didn't realize was the power of the conversations that take place between sessions. Funny enough, it's come to be the space I remember most, organizing and conducting interviews for the highlight videos. More and more we're seeing MCN provide opportunities for people to learn beyond traditional conference formats. There's something for everyone, because everyone is able—and encouraged—to speak up and take action. Look no further than the session, "Don't Retweet This: Social Media Open Mic 3.0 (UNCONFERENCE)."[6] What started as a happy hour for social media managers turned into an unconference session that's taken place the past three years—with new hosts continuing the conversation this past year.

These in-between sessions are powerful because they fuse the energy of the Ignite talks with trade-speak, social justice with academic rigor, professional development with community activism. At MCN there's room for everyone to get involved and lend their voice/experience in order to help create opportunities to learn. We're able to develop our ideas to a greater extent, in the company of collaborators. I can confidently say that MCN helped me develop, and continues to enhance, my professional skill set. Part of that has to do with my involvement with the organization. The role has brought its challenges, but it's ultimately given me a lens through which to watch this rapidly changing field. We talk about humanizing the museum, but really, we're humanizing the humans in the museums. Through empathy trainings, therapy sessions, and tons of PowerPoint slides, together we present in those often-wacky named rooms with and for our colleagues, all the while empowering each other to leave the conference more enlightened and uplifted than when we first arrived. It's precisely for these reasons that as someone who now works tangentially to the field in higher education, it is easy to come back to my annual winter camp for cultural organizations.

NOTES

1. Museum Computer Network, MCN 2015 Highlights, *YouTube*, 7 Nov. 2015, www.youtube.com/watch?v=3i7WBYCr208 (accessed February 19, 2019).

2. "Chatham House Rules," *Chatham House*, The Royal Institute of International Affairs, Dec. 7, 2018, http://www.chathamhouse.org/chatham-house-rule (accessed February 16, 2019).

3. Adrienne Lalli Hills and Seema Rao, "Humanizing the Un-conference: Get the Lead Out!," Unconference Session, *Museum Computer Network Conference*, Denver, CO, 2018.

4. Amanda Dearolph, Carissa Dougherty, Ellice Engdahl, Mark McKay, Victoria Portway, and Lisel Record, "The In-Between: How to facilitate interdepartmental collaboration from the institutional middle," Conference Presentation, *Museum Computer Network Conference*, Denver, CO, 2018, https://bit.ly/2Yh5eLl (accessed February 19, 2019).

5. Susan Edwards, Michele Grohe, and Kathryn Quigley, " Talk to Your Visitors: DIY Human-Centered Research," Conference Presentation, *Museum Computer Network Conference*, Denver, CO, 2018, https://bit.ly/2Yg11Hp (accessed February 19, 2019).

6. Alex Light and Jonathan Munar, "Don't Retweet This: Social Media Open Mic 3.0 (UNCONFERENCE)," Conference Presentation, *Museum Computer Network Conference*, Denver, CO, 2018, https://bit.ly/2umBLl6 (accessed February 19, 2019).

BIBLIOGRAPHY

"Chatham House Rules." *Chatham House*. The Royal Institute of International Affairs, Dec. 7, 2018, http://www.chathamhouse.org/chatham-house-rule (accessed February 16, 2019).

Dearolph, Amanda, Carissa Dougherty, Ellice Engdahl, Mark McKay, Victoria Portway, and Lisel Record. "The In-Between: How to facilitate interdepartmental collaboration from the institutional middle." Conference Presentation. *Museum Computer Network Conference*, Denver, CO, 2018. https://bit.ly/2Yh5eLl (accessed February 19, 2019).

Edwards, Susan, Michele Grohe, and Kathryn Quigley. "Talk to Your Visitors: DIY Human-Centered Research." Conference Presentation. *Museum Computer Network Conference*, Denver, CO, 2018. https://bit.ly/2Yg11Hp (accessed February 19, 2019).

Hills, Adrienne Lalli and Seema Rao. "Humanizing the Un-conference: Get the Lead Out!." Unconference Session. *Museum Computer Network Conference*, Denver, CO, 2018.

Light, Alex, and Jonathan Munar. "Don't Retweet This: Social Media Open Mic 3.0 (UNCONFERENCE)." Conference Presentation. *Museum Computer Network Conference*, Denver, CO, 2018. https://bit.ly/2umBLl6 (accessed February 19, 2019).

Museum Computer Network. MCN 2015 Highlights. *YouTube*. 7 Nov. 2015, https://www.youtube.com/watch?v=3i7WBYCr208 (accessed February 19, 2019).

Chapter 5

Cultural Spaces After the Internet

Meagan Estep
Marty Spellerberg

In November 2018, thirty people came together in Denver for a roundtable discussion called "Proud to Be Flesh: Cultural Spaces After the Internet" as part of the MCN conference. Both authors participated in the conversation and build on the issues raised in this essay.

"Proud to be flesh." This was the tagline of *Mute*, a magazine founded in 1994—when the World Wide Web was newborn—to discuss the interrelationship of art and new technologies.[1] This phrase captures the frisson that our physical experience is now distinct from another possible way of being. That the flesh matters, *still*.

In the flesh, a museum visitor can slow down and find the space to have a transformative experience. Magic can happen when visitors spend time observing, contemplating, and really drinking in an object in a museum. Scholar David Carr calls this "becoming"[2]—in other words, we can use objects as powerful teachers of something new. They transport us, add depth and dimension to our lives, and stir our emotions.

It's not new to say that there is no "best" way to engage with objects in a museum.[3] Nor can we say the best way to observe or connect with a museum online. Things have changed since 1994, especially in the online experience of museums, which can no longer be considered entirely separate from the on-site. As much of the world moves online, what's next for engaging, enriching, in-real-life experiences of art and culture?[4]

Curators might say that you still need an in-real-life experience, along with some type of scholarly information, to access an aesthetic experience. Educators might tell you that you need a participatory tour (or two) and a lot of open-ended questions. An artist or creator might ask you to quietly contemplate their object, be it online or on-site.

With both digital and physical experiences blended in a museum setting, can we even distinguish one from the other? Are they even separate?

According to *Art In America*, "It's no longer a question of whether art institutions should have a virtual presence. Rather, the onus is being placed on designers to facilitate meaningful interactions with art that might occur in the gallery, via Web-based applications or in new hybrid spaces that merge the real and the virtual."[5]

What is different about these spaces from the ones that came before?

Let's look to the example of a digital-native. *Artsy* bills itself as a "place to learn about and collect art online." Rather than a having an online office within a larger offline organization, they've flipped the ratios. Their "special projects" initiative applies online resources toward offline activations. For example, the decision to work with artist Misha Kahn on an offline project, a Tiki Bar during Frieze New York,[6] followed from the success of an online profile. "We knew that he had resonated with our online audience and would likely excite our offline audience as well," they explained.[7]

Or consider artists such as Kara Walker, whose work is so prolific on Instagram, a social-media platform, that some people skipped seeing a piece because they felt that they had already sufficiently experienced it. As Sarah Hromack, then director of digital media at the Whitney, reported:

> *I witnessed a conversation wherein a handful of New York-based arts professionals admitted to having willfully refrained from seeing Kara Walker's recent installation,* A Subtlety, or the Marvelous Sugar Baby—*a magnificent larger-than-life sphinx made of refined white sugar*—*in Brooklyn's Domino Sugar factory, because they felt that they had already sufficiently experienced the piece through images seen in others' Instagram feeds.*[8]

The social media presence of this piece spawned a discussion of issues of race[9] and sexuality[10] in the public's engagement with art. Keeping her focus trained on the apparent either/or of online/offline visitation, Hromack continued,

> To think that now, in 2014, we would allow ourselves to be dissuaded from a physical experience by the effects of a digital interface is sad ... Seeing an image pop up over and over again in various social media feeds might make me feel a sense of familiarity with the work, but it cannot approximate my sensorial experience—and I say this as a person that has experienced augmented and virtual reality in military-grade computer labs![11]

What may have been an obvious, settled fact in 2014 became less-so four years later, when the *New York Times* was compelled to ask: "Does the availability of virtual reality tours, videos and photographs of museum collections worldwide make physical museums themselves obsolete?"[12]

Of what a visitor may find within museum walls, they write:

> In the presence of the "Mona Lisa," digital photography, more than looking at the actual artwork, has become the primary experience. ... The way the "Mona Lisa" is viewed is, in fact, soberingly representative of the way most art is viewed in today's saturated, digitally mediated, visual culture. How many more (or fewer) seconds do cellphone-wielding visitors spend looking at individual works at a commercial art fair or exhibition than at the Louvre? How is an artistic reputation made these days, other than through Instagram?[13]

A condition to which the *New Yorker* attempts to ascribe meaning:

> Visual art in 2018 is increasingly a set piece of sorts, an aesthetic signifier that can mean "taste," or "contemplation," or "having a good time," depending on the artwork in question. Rothko paintings are particularly good for this, judging by their popularity online; they flatten easily into bright swaths of color, while maintaining a certain cultural cachet.[14]

In response, new "museums" have emerged, like the Color Factory in New York[15] or the Museum of Ice Cream in San Francisco,[16] boasting installations that entice visitors to take pictures of their experiences.

> What the creators of these experiences have realized is that a lot of people want to take pictures of themselves in a museum, without going to a traditional museum. So they've created temporary, overstuffed spaces that are geared toward online aesthetics and in-real-life consumption.[17]

Meow Wolf established itself in 2008 as an art collective. The group "creates immersive and interactive experiences that transport audiences of all ages into fantastic realms of story and exploration."[18] These artists take care to be seen as creating legitimate works of contemporary art. The collective's 20,000-square-foot *House of Eternal Return* in Santa Fe "aims to offer more than just photo ops."

Rather, (Founder Vince) Kadlubek and his colleagues are working towards a future where high-quality, thought-provoking art environments are the norm. ... Meow Wolf took cues from other buzz-worthy immersive art experiences—like Kusama's "Infinity Rooms," James Turrell's light installations, and enveloping animations by teamLAB. "We've been inspired by them because they showcased credibility in this type of space," Kadlubek explained. But at its core, Meow Wolf has looked to fellow collectives—like Wham City in Baltimore and the Do LaB in Los Angeles—as well as the art that gets made annually at the Burning Man festival.[19]

To the *Times*, however, such efforts represent an "existential void":

> The most that these spaces can offer is the facsimile of traditional pleasures. They take nature and art and knowledge seeking, flatten them into sight gags and stick them to every stray surface. ... Observing a work of art or climbing a mountain actually invites us to create meaning in our lives. But in these spaces, the idea of "interacting" with the world is made so slickly transactional that our role is hugely diminished.[20]

We suggest that it can be more than that. Deeply engaging experiences can look different for each visitor; no one way is right or wrong. Who are we, as museum professionals, to decide how another person should make meaning during their experience?

In his 2009 book, *Identity and the Museum Visitor Experience*, John Falk evaluates motivations behind a visitor's experience. He outlines a series of specific reasons given by visitors for choosing to attend a museum, based on their needs and values.[21] Some enjoy reading wall text, some enjoy wandering aimlessly; some like to travel in packs of friends and talk the entire time; others use the museum as a contemplative space. No one type of visitor motivation has greater value over any other. Nor does a visitor own only one identity type—in fact, motivations might change by day or mood.

The 2017 Culture Track report noted that museum-goers preferred to be "entertained" rather than "educated" and wanted more "social interactions" as opposed to "quiet reflection" when they visited exhibitions.[22] Our own research into the motivations of museum website visitors is analogous, with overall strong support for "social" visitation.[23] Additionally, an overwhelming majority of participants in the Culture Track study wanted digital experiences in museums.[24]

Can people connect with a work of art through a photo or a selfie? Museum experience designer Jim Fishwick says yes. "This is the social function of photography," he explains, "rather than an exercise in vanity."[25]

By extending the museum experience to their devices, visitors are creating external hard drives of their memories. Experiences are captured, saved, preserved. A thoughtful observer can detect both fun and thought in how people have staged, designed, and creatively constructed their feeds. These visitors are assembling their own experiences, not following expectations of what a traditional museum experience should be.

Online and in-real-life now occur simultaneously, in concert. Facilitating your experience with a device has no bearing on its depth. Using your phone mediates your experience in a museum—and that's okay. Mediated experiences look different for every visitor.

In the end, museums must be open to experiences of all kinds, whether they are onsite, online, object-based, or experiential. After all, not every experience with an object will be transformative—and not every object-based experience will be in front of an object.

We—as artists, technologists, educators—should be open to letting our visitors discover meaning on their own terms, from their own points of view, and through their own technological lenses.

NOTES

1. "Proud to Be Flesh - a Mute Magazine Anthology," *Mute,* http://www.metamute.org/shop/mute-books/proud-to-be-flesh-mute-magazine-anthology (accessed February 14, 2019).

2. "Six Questions with Dr. David Carr," *Smithsonian Libraries Unbound*, February 2, 2015, https://blog.library.si.edu/blog/2015/02/11/six-questions-with-dr-david-carr/ (accessed February 14, 2019).

3. Elena Goukassian, "Is There a Right Way to Look at Art?," *Hyperallergic*, January 8, 2018, https://hyperallergic.com/416912/is-there-a-right-way-to-look-at-art/ (Accessed March 1, 2019).

4. Elena Soboleva, "The Power of Taking an Online Arts Platform Offline," *Medium*, November 22, 2016, https://medium.com/artsy-blog/how-an-online-platform-empowers-artists-irl-d52aefe373ca (accessed February 14, 2019).

5. Rob Giampietro and Sarah Hromack, "The Museum Interface," *Art in America*, Sep 29, 2014, https://www.artinamericamagazine.com/news-features/magazines/the-museum-interface/ (accessed February 14, 2019).

6. Olivia Martin, "Paradise found: Artsy and Misha Kahn turn Sixty LES bar into living art,"

Wallpaper, May 6, 2016, https://www.wallpaper.com/art/paradise-found-artsy-and-misha-kahn-turn-sixty-hotels-tiki-tabu-bar-into-a-living-art-installation (accessed March 1, 2019).

7.   Elena Soboleva, "The Power of Taking an Online Arts Platform Offline," *Medium*, November 22, 2016, https://medium.com/artsy-blog/how-an-online-platform-empowers-artists-irl-d52aefe373ca (accessed February 14, 2019).

8.   Giampietro and Hromack, "The Museum Interface."

9.   Jamilah King, "The Overwhelming Whiteness of Black Art," *Colorlines,* May 21, 2014, https://www.colorlines.com/articles/overwhelming-whiteness-black-art (accessed March 1, 2019).

10.   Cait Munro, "Kara Walker's Sugar Sphinx Spawns Offensive Instagram Photos," *Artnet*, May 30, 2014, https://news.artnet.com/exhibitions/kara-walkers-sugar-sphinx-spawns-offensive-instagram-photos-29989 (accessed March 1, 2019).

11.   Ibid.

12.   Michael Gonchar, "Are Museums Still Important in the Digital Age?," *The New York Times*, September 11, 2018, https://www.nytimes.com/2018/09/11/learning/museums-protection-internet.html (accessed February 14, 2019).

13.   Scott Reyburn, "What the Mona Lisa Tells Us About Art in the Instagram Era," *The New York Times*, April 27, 2018, https://www.nytimes.com/2018/04/27/arts/design/mona-lisa-instagram-art.html (accessed February 14, 2019).

14.   Sophie Haigney, "The Museums of Instagram," *The New Yorker*, September 16, 2018, https://www.newyorker.com/culture/culture-desk/the-museums-of-instagram (accessed February 14, 2019).

15.   "Color Factory," *Instagram*, https://www.instagram.com/colorfactoryco/ (accessed February 14, 2019).

16.   "Museum of Ice Cream," *Instagram*, https://www.instagram.com/museumoficecream (accessed February 14, 2019).

17.   Haigney, "The Museums of Instagram."

18.   "Our Story," *Meow Wolf,* https://meowwolf.com/about (accessed March 1, 2019).

19.   Casey Lesser, "A New Breed of Immersive Art Experiences Offers a Gateway to Alternative Realities," *Medium*, May 21, 2018, https://www.artsy.net/article/artsy-editorial-new-breed-immersive-art-experiences-offers-gateway-alternative-realities (accessed February 14, 2019).

20.   Amanda Hess, "The Existential Void of the Pop-Up 'Experience'," *The New York Times*, September 26, 2018, https://www.nytimes.com/2018/09/26/arts/color-factory-museum-of-ice-cream-rose-mansion-29rooms-candytopia.html (accessed February 14, 2019).

21.   John H. Falk, *Identity and the Museum Visitor Experience* (Walnut Creek, CA: Left Coast Press, 2009), 35.

22. "Culture Track '17," *La Placa Cohen*, https://culturetrack.com/reports (accessed February 13, 2019).

23. Sarah Wambold and Marty Spellerberg, "Identity-related motivations online: Falk's framework applied to US museum websites," *Journal of Digital & Social Media Marketing,* Volume 5 Number 4 (Spring 2018).

24. "Culture Track '17."

25. Jim Fishwick, "Proud to be Flesh: Cultural Spaces After the Internet," Roundtable conversation, *Museum Computer Network Conference*, Denver, CO, 2018.

BIBLIOGRAPHY

"Color Factory (@colorfactoryco)." *Instagram*. https://www.instagram.com/colorfactoryco/ (accessed February 14, 2019).

"Culture Track Reports | Explore Culture Track Reports from Years past." *Culture Track*. https://culturetrack.com/reports (accessed February 13, 2019).

"Museum of Ice Cream (@museumoficecream)." *Instagram*. https://www.instagram.com/museumoficecream/ (accessed February 14, 2019).

"Our Story." *Meow Wolf*. https://meowwolf.com/about (accessed March 1, 2019).

"Proud to Be Flesh - a Mute Magazine Anthology." *Mute*. http://www.metamute.org/shop/mute-books/proud-to-be-flesh-mute-magazine-anthology (accessed February 14, 2019).

"Six Questions with Dr. David Carr." *Smithsonian Libraries Unbound*. https://blog.library.si.edu/blog/2015/02/11/six-questions-with-dr-david-carr/ (accessed February 14, 2019).

Falk, John Howard. *Identity and the Museum Visitor Experience*. Walnut Creek, CA: Left Coast Press, 2009.

Fishwick, Jim. "Proud to be Flesh: Cultural Spaces After the Internet." Roundtable conversation. *Museum Computer Network*, Denver, CO, 2018.

Giampietro, Rob, and Sarah Hromack. "The Museum Interface." *Art in America*. September 29, 2014.

Gonchar, Michael. "Are Museums Still Important in the Digital Age?." *The New York Times*. September 11, 2008. https://www.nytimes.com/2018/09/11/learning/museums-protection-internet.html (accessed February 14, 2019).

Goukassian, Elena. "Is There a Right Way to Look at Art?." *Hyperallergic*. January 09, 2018. https://hyperallergic.com/416912/is-there-a-right-way-to-look-at-art/ (accessed March 1, 2019).

Haigney, Sophie. "The Museums of Instagram." *The New Yorker*. September 16, 2018.

Hess, Amanda. "The Existential Void of the Pop-Up 'Experience'." *The New York Times*. September 26, 2018. https://www.nytimes.com/2018/09/26/arts/color-factory-museum-of-ice-cream-rose-mansion-29rooms-candytopia.html (accessed February 14, 2019).

King, Jamilah. "The Overwhelming Whiteness of Black Art." *Colorlines*. May 21, 2014. https://www.colorlines.com/articles/overwhelming-whiteness-black-art (accessed March 1, 2019).

Lesser, Casey. "A New Breed of Immersive Art Experiences Offers a Gateway to Alternative Realities." *Artsy*. May 21, 2018. https://www.artsy.net/article/artsy-editorial-new-breed-immersive-art-experiences-offers-gateway-alternative-realities (accessed February 14, 2019).

Martin, Olivia. "Paradise Found: Artsy and Misha Kahn Turn Sixty LES Bar into Living Art." *Wallpaper*, May 6, 2016.

Munro, Cait. "Offensive Instagram Pics Plague Walker's Sphinx." *Artnet News*. May 30, 2014. https://news.artnet.com/exhibitions/kara-walkers-sugar-sphinx-spawns-offensive-instagram-photos-29989 (accessed March 01, 2019).

Reyburn, Scott. "What the Mona Lisa Tells Us About Art in the Instagram Era." *The New York Times*, April 27, 2018. https://www.nytimes.com/2018/04/27/arts/design/mona-lisa-instagram-art.html (accessed February 14, 2019).

Soboleva, Elena. "The Power of Taking an Online Arts Platform Offline." *Medium*. November 22, 2016. https://medium.com/artsy-blog/how-an-online-platform-empowers-artists-irl-d52aefe373ca (accessed February 14, 2019).

Wambold, Sarah, and Martin Spellerberg. "Identity-related Motivations Online: Falk's Framework Applied to US Museum Websites." *Journal of Digital & Social Media Marketing* 5, no. 4 (Spring 2018).

Chapter 6

Humanizing Augmented Reality with Lumin

Megan DiRienzo
Andrea Montiel de Shuman
Alicia Viera

Art museums are packed with objects that connect us to the creativity of human beings from around the globe and throughout time. So, why—in this media-saturated world that confuses fiction with fact—would museums choose to disrupt this authentic connection to humanity with a handheld device that *augments* reality? The formative evaluation of *Lumin,* an augmented reality (AR) tour at the Detroit Institute of Arts (DIA), revealed some compelling reasons.

The three-year project put the visitor first, including evaluation at every development phase to garner feedback about content and usability. The evaluation findings provided a cache of useful data that, together with critical self-reflection on our interpretive practice, guided the *Lumin* team through the development of 12 AR prototype experiences (Figure 1).

Figure 1 Visitors use Lumin–an app on a held hand device–to view digital objects in AR.

The Potential of AR

AR allows us to place digital objects over real objects, or anywhere around us. The ability to insert digital artworks, game experiences, content overlays and/or live dinosaurs into the museum is enticing. However, we found that in order to create impactful experiences, the endless possibilities of AR need to be strategically pared down into engagements that weave together human-centered functionality and human-centered content.

Re-learning Human Behavior

The first evaluation report completed in the spring of 2017 revealed that AR required visitors to use handheld devices in unfamiliar ways. Visitors were pinching and zooming expecting an up-close view of an AR object. But because Lumin AR objects behave like "real" objects, visitors had to physically move the device toward objects for a closer look (Figure 2). They also found it unintuitive to explore their surroundings with the device, typically missing digital objects placed above or behind them (Figure 3).

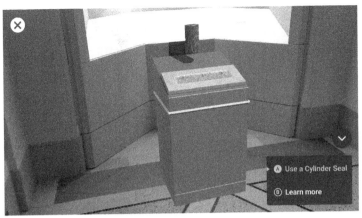

Figure 2 Visitors who wanted a closer look at this animated cylinder seal often tried to pinch and zoom, rather than moving their devices closer to the virtual object.

Figure 3 The prototype experience about this altarpiece required visitors to search the gallery for the three highlighted works. Content messages were not communicated through the gaming experience, which visitors found confusing.

Those who quickly picked up the unfamiliar behaviors had an easier time engaging with AR experiences. But visitors who did not adapt to them, either missed the full experience or had to request assistance from others. The team tested a number of solutions to this problem, including a training game about unfamiliar behaviors and written directions telling visitors where to look or go. Visitors reported that neither approach completely compensated for the unfamiliar functionality.

Respecting human behavior is key to creating an effortless experience, so we stripped away complex gaming elements, aligned digital objects within obvious sightlines, and carefully sized and placed digital objects in ways that did not require moving closer to appreciate details.

Although we experimented with AR's full potential in a number of stops, the most impactful prototypes had the simplest functionality, allowing visitors to focus on the surprising human connections AR can reveal rather than navigating its unintuitive aspects.

Humanizing AR Content

Artworks that are functional, have hidden or unseen elements, or once existed in a time or place remote from the here and now had the deepest impact on visitors according to our findings. The examples below highlight our three most successful prototype AR experiences.

AR Shows Objects in Action

Two marble jar stands, called *kilgas*, are displayed in a dark passageway toward the back of the Islamic World galleries at the DIA. School children on tours often giggle when they see them, thinking they are toilets. In actuality, *kilgas* hold water filtration jars. Impurities are filtered out of the water as it seeps through the jar's pores and drips into the bowl of the *kilga*. Revealing the filtration process through traditional media like photos or video isn't possible because few jars have survived. Placing a virtual *kilga*, complete with a functional jar and the sound of water drops, next to the real *kilgas* brought the purification system to life, connecting visitors with the universal need for cool, clean water (Figure 4).

Figure 4 An animation is worth 1000 words. Lumin helps visitors understand the purpose of a *kilga*.

AR Reveals Unseen Humanity

AR presented the opportunity to help visitors recognize the mummy at the DIA as a human rather than an intriguing artifact. GuidiGo's animators created a three-dimensional reconstruction of the person's skeleton based on x-rays the DIA had taken a number of years ago. When viewed in AR, the 3D model is overlaid on the mummy, driving the point home that it's a human! The team was surprised by the visitors' response to the experience with comments like, "There's a person in there!?" The Lumin stop physically demonstrates the mummy's humanity and includes text overlays that share what little the DIA knows about the man's life (Figure 5).

Figure 5 Lumin shows visitors there is an actual person inside the mummy.

AR Melds the Past and Present

The Ishtar gate leading into the ancient city of Babylon was adorned with dozens of mosaics depicting fierce creatures. The DIA has one of these mosaics displayed in a central location, holding together a gallery space that explores empire building in the ancient Middle East. An immersive recreation of the Ishtar Gate viewed through the *Lumin* device allows visitors to experience the sense of grandeur likely felt by the people entering the ancient metropolis (Figure 6).

Figure 6 Visitor is about to walk through the virtual reproduction of the Ishtar gate.

Experiences to Share

Although there is much we are still discovering, we hope that the lessons we learned during the development of *Lumin* will be valuable to museum professionals as they embark on their own AR journeys. Here are five major insights from our prototype project.

Key Insights:

1. **Plan for sustainability**. As technology and tools evolve by the day, it is important to evaluate the opportunities and limitations of what is available at hand in different phases of the project. Some things we were not able to do in the first prototype we were able to accomplish in the second because of how the tools upgraded.

2. **Design in three dimensions, but don't assume your visitors will think spatially**. It is crucial to consider the positioning and movements of the user in relation to physical and digital objects. Visitors aren't used to looking up and around for content, so position digital objects in plain sight or give a strong visual clue to move.

3. **Acknowledge that AR is exhausting**. Figuring out how to engage with a digital object that behaves as a real object is foreign and demands extra effort from the user. Focus on reducing the number of steps to an experience, simplifying the interface, balancing engagement levels, and strategizing content to fit natural user behavior and avoid sensory overload.

4. **Avoid thinking you know your audience**. Tech fans won't be the only ones trying new technology. Focus on broad accessibility principles like large font, clear icons, and intuitive user flows. Research findings can help negotiate with developers when there are changes needed to platforms.

5. **You might not need AR**. Resist the temptation to invest in assuming that innovation requires the latest, flashiest technology. AR projects can be costly in the budget and human resources. Use AR where the limitations of reality results in specific, addressable visitor needs.

The *Lumin* team looks forward to sharing the summative evaluation report at MCN after the polished experience debuts to the public in April of this year.

Chapter 7

Performing the Museum: Applying a Visitor-Centered Approach to Strategy, Experience and Interactions

Seema Rao
Jim Fishwick
Alli Burness

Just as gender and identity are performative for individuals, so too is the institutional act of 'being' a museum through programming, interpretation and communications. Authentic, relevant and accessible exchanges require meeting people where they are, connecting with visitors personally, understanding the communication tropes they use and their definition of what art or culture may be to them. This chapter is speculative in that we explore the performative museum as a concept and discuss methods to apply it within organizations. First, we discuss the concept at a theoretical and strategic level by focussing on the values that museums can realise as an outcome. Then, we explore how the concept can manifest as a unified and felt experience through signage and behavioural rules that clearly articulate the museum's values to visitors. Lastly, we outline some practical improvisation techniques that can be used to flexibly build interactions with visitors and achieve empathy in an organization's body language.

The concepts underlying this work grew from a presentation at the 2016 Museum Computer Network conference by a group of museum professionals exploring the impact of visitor social photography on the museum. Alli Burness, Jenny Kidd, Megan Estep and Chad Weinard took inspiration from in-progress research examining datasets of Instagram images taken by visitors to the Museum of Contemporary Art in Sydney, Australia and similar research conducted at the Museum of Islamic Art in Doha, Qatar.[1] The authors of both sets of research emphasized that social photography can allow visitors to express their agency and authority through sharing their embodied experiences of museums. At its heart, the framework developed by Burness, Kidd, Estep and Weinard defined the museum as a relationship between an organization and its visitors (Figure 1).[2]

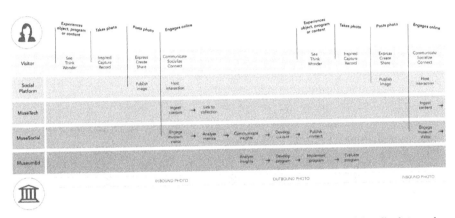

Figure 1 The Museum Social Photo Journey, a conceptual framework outlining how a social media photograph posted by a visitor might impact and inform a response from a museum.

Two years later, our understanding has deepened. We now believe the museum can be defined as a particular type of relationship. In this chapter, we argue that museums are sites of performative exchange created through interaction and emerge through the experience of 'doing the museum'. In this way, museums can be reframed as performative rather than authoritative. They begin to exist when visitors interact with the museum and the museum interacts with visitors through organizational body language. While we argue for the performative museum in this chapter, we advocate against the museum as a performance and the rise of Instagram museums.[3] The museum is created in the moment of an experience shared by an organization and the visitor, triggered by an interaction. This can then be *expressed* in the form of social photography but cannot be encapsulated within a photograph itself.

It is useful to understand the distinction between the terms 'performance' and 'performativity'. A 'performance' is a noun. It is an act that can stand on its own. In contrast, 'performativity' is a concept that describes behaviours that are repeated. Judith Butler has defined this as "not a singular act, but a repetition and a ritual, which achieves its effects through its naturalisation in the context of a body."[4] By this we understand Butler to mean that a performative act is one that is constantly repeated, perhaps as a ritual that brings a religion to life, or a behaviour that brings an identity or social role into being. It is through performative acts that we construct our identities and social groups.

We can scale up Butler's concept of individual performativity by applying Chris Flink's concept of organizational body language.[5] Flink refers to the power of the form, shape, functionality and aesthetics of a space to reflect values that have the ability to shape the experience of a person. By extension, the actions and behaviours of people who represent an organization extend that power. The grammar of a museum's buildings, spaces, lighting, signage, furniture and labels create a stage on which the interactions, tone, voice and responsiveness of staff within it are performed. Together these form the organizational body language of a museum.

The performative museum is formed by repeatedly exchanging interactions with visitors that evolve the values and identity of both the visitor and the organization. This is a challenging concept, but it is gaining traction in the cultural sector. Research by Jay Rounds indicates that visitors use museums primarily for identity-work, or "the processes through which we construct, maintain, and adapt our sense of personal identity, and persuade other people to believe in that identity."[6] At Communicating the Museum conference in 2014, Kingsley Jayasekera described the museum as "a relationship between content and an audience."[7] In 2016, Alli Burness has laid theoretical groundwork that positions selfies taken in museums is a response to and form of self-expression inspired by museum objects.[8] In 2018, James Bradburne marked the distinction between enacting a collection and holding objects in a collection.[9] Increasingly, leaders in the cultural sector are understanding and articulating the performative nature of the museum and the ways in which this can be observed.

Intentionally applying the concept of the performative museum involves different approaches at the strategic, experiential and interactional levels. To effect such a change at a strategic level, we should understand where an organization is currently, where it needs to move to and how to get there. We can apply a type of design reasoning to this by seeing these as *elements* of an organization now, the *outcome* the organization is seeking to achieve and the *pattern of relationships* or interactions it uses to get there.[10] How do these three settings in our reasoning need to shift to realise the performative museum?

Our hypothesis in this chapter is that to achieve belonging and identity-work as a shared outcome for both visitors and the museum, we should reframe the relationship through which museums engage with visitors. The museum moves *from* a trusted authority that aims for educational and inspirational outcomes, *to* a performative relationship of exchange for the shared outcomes of belonging and identity work (Figure 2). It is this intentional outcome (the values of belonging and identity-work) that should be routinely enacted by the physical and digital infrastructure of a museum, as well as staff and visitors.

From	To
To achieve the outcome of EDUCATION & INSPIRATION	To achieve the outcome of BELONGING & IDENTITY-WORK
Relationship to achieve it MUSEUM AS A TRUSTED AUTHORITY	Relationship to achieve it MUSEUM AS A PERFORMATIVE EXCHANGE
What are the priority elements? • EXHIBITIONS & COLLECTIONS • PUBLISHING • EVENTS & PUBLIC PROGRAMS	What are the priority elements? • INTERACTIONS • EVENTS & PUBLIC PROGRAMS • EXHIBITIONS & COLLECTIONS

Figure 2 The strategic shifts involved in moving from the museum as a trusted authority to the museum as a performative exchange

This reframing re-prioritises the activities, or elements, of a museum. Rather than focussing on exhibitions, collections or publications as means for disseminating information, the performative museum will leverage exhibitions, the collection or publications *in service of* experiences that facilitate interactions with visitors. Education and inspiration remain present, but in the performative museum, they work as sites of experience, as vehicles enabling interactions that build a sense of belonging.

If organizational values are shared with visitors, and the elements of experience that enact them are interconnected, their outcome can be powerfully achieved. However, the perception of an experience is often subliminal. Experience often only touches the conscious mind when errors or lapses occur. Who has not noticed a jarring element in a space, like the shining red exit sign in an elegant Victorian house museum? To become intuitive, experience requires systematic intentional thought to interconnect all the elements of an institution.

Good experience is easy to feel but sometimes hard to describe. In practice, experience requires strategic awareness and implementation, so every element is produced to stay in line with the organization's cultural norms, philosophical underpinnings, and intended visitor experience. Said differently, all staff need to put in thought to the experience so visitors will feel the organization's values, even if unconsciously. Ideally, every organization should articulate how their visitor should feel in their space. If we think of an organization as a system of decisions, the experience level is the benchmark against which all choices are made. An organization can decide their brand experience is relaxed curiosity, for example, based on their institutional values of education and lively learning. All choices from the font on signs to the types of programs would be measured against the defined experience.

Museums often overlook the simple task of articulating the quality of their intended experience and instead, are more focused on what the visitor should think. However, when visitor's feelings are ignored, spaces leave visitors feeling cold or unwelcome and unable to think at all. By focusing on shared values, museums can build visitor needs and feelings into their work of connecting visitors with collections and community.

Physical space is the easiest way to consider experience. Signage is the most common site of experience dissonance in museums. It is often produced in design departments, with the text being determined by marketing or education. These departments, however, often ignore the feelings that such signs produce in visitors. Signs are then produced to follow the design norms of the institution. Art museums, particularly, institute subtle norms, in keeping with their near clinical spaces. Subtle signs work in spaces where the message is redundant, and users already know the information. For example, apartment buildings often place simple, subtle signs to remind inhabitants of garbage day. However, art museum patrons, in large part, don't know the information in the signs. Consider the subtle 'no food or drink the gallery' signs that museums use during parties and late-night events. Staff are almost always stationed with those signs because no one reads them. Human nature certainly comes into play, in this case. However, the design of these signs is also to blame. Signs cannot communicate if they are produced to be hidden in plain sight.

When an unnamed museum created list of rules for an education and technology space, the decision was made to place these rules in white text on glass with the intention of maintaining the sanctity of the space. Explicitly articulated rules, it should be said, was a significant move by the museum towards improving visitor experience. Prior to that time, leadership staff had argued that posting the rules felt punitive. We argue museums have rules, posted or not. Implied rules are no less punitive and serve to support the general cultural inaccessibility that can plague such organizations. However, the unexpected message of producing signage in this manner was that the rules were unimportant. Spaces that want visitors to read the rules make them clear and legible.

At the Phoenix Museum of Art, "Do Not Touch" signs are an example of placing the importance of the message over the unspoken rules of design (Figure 3). Produced in bright colors, their large stanchion signs were positioned throughout the galleries. The signs are notable not just for their placement in the center of galleries and for their appealing colors. The team at Phoenix Museum of Art took great effort to communicate not just the rules but the organization's attitude toward patrons with open, inviting language. These signs are a stellar example of an organization working across silos to deliver a unified experience to patrons as manifest in physical artifacts of the space, in this case, a sign.

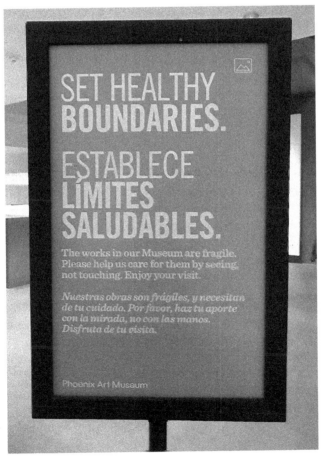

Figure 3 Signage at the Phoenix Museum of Art conveyed a deliberate tone that aligns with the values of the organization, including in the colours and fonts used.

Spaces and signage are some of the easiest ways for organizations to improve the experience level. However, for visitors, the experience level is most apparent in interactions with staff. Any person going to Disney World or a similar leisure space intuitively understands their staff interactions in delivering elements of the experience level. The staff have specific codified behavioral norms. While museums might not want to be as circumscribed as corporate experiences, the idea of developing norms for visitor experience is rare in museums. Front of house staff are the greatest ambassadors if museums take the effort to leverage their skills and powerful position in meaningful visitor experience.

There are lots of ways that interactions might be mediated as part of a museum experience. These could include a public program, an exhibition, front-of-house staff or a twitter campaign. Museum experiences are a unique challenge because they usually give visitors a free choice of what to do. Unlike tightly-crafted forms of performance like opera or film, the performative museum experience (especially exhibition-based ones) allow visitors to construct their visit as they go. This very aspect makes museums a rich medium for visitors to do identity work. Visitors might choose to walk clockwise around a room, or anti-clockwise. They might stop in the middle and look at one work for an hour, or skip a room entirely, or document their visit on their Instagram story, or propose marriage to their partner. The balance between what a museum intends and how a visitor applies their agency is constantly shifting.

Museum experiences emerge in the moment, out of a series of spontaneous decisions made by the visitor in response to what they see, hear and feel around them. In a way, this is improvisation. Like improvised theatre, where performers create scenes and stories by responding to and building on each other's ideas, the visitor and the museum are working together by performing identity-driven roles to create the museum experience. Using the lens of improvisation can help us better understand and design for this kind of flexibility and empathy in museums.

The foundational philosophy of improvisation is 'yes and'. Collaborative stories get told faster if you agree with the information your partner contributes, known as their *offer*, and then build on it. Each *offer* builds on the previous one.[11] When visitors come to a museum, they see a range of *offers* in the form of an exhibition, a screening, a talk, a café. They 'yes and' that offer by going to the exhibition, for instance, and responding to it emotionally, intellectually, socially. But how do museums then 'yes and' their offer in return, building on the exchange to achieve shared values?

A hypothetical example will help us to unpack how to achieve this. Let's say there is a large diamond on display. A visitor might respond by expressing interest in its shape or colour. They might wonder about its crystal structure. They might be angered by the structural injustices of the diamond industry. These are all valid and authentic responses. The staff member in the room can build on their reaction of "I love how sparkly it is!" by responding with, "Well, we have a whole wall of glittery things in the next room."

We can also go below surface readings of what people say to deduce the drivers or motivation behind them. In improvisation this is called the offer behind the offer. Someone who responds to the diamond by saying "my grandfather had one like that" is also signalling that they are interested in heirlooms and social history. A staff member might respond by pointing them to other objects in the exhibition that have interesting family lineages.

By responding to 'the offer behind the offer,' we move from responding to what visitors say towards responding to their motivations and drivers. For instance, if a visitor is about to touch an off-limits sculpture, that suggests they want to get closer to it or understand more about it. A museum staff member can 'yes and' this offer by telling them more about its materials, about its fragility, about the oil in their fingers. The visitor gets 'closer' to the object, without us having to file an incident report with the conservation department. In this way, conversation aids conservation and builds shared values.

The importance of visitor motivation is already well established in the cultural sector. Both John Falk's analysis of visitor motivations and Culture Segments developed by Morris Hargreaves McIntyre gather visitors into broad groups based on what they want from cultural experiences.[12] The challenge faced by the performative museum is to bring the motivations of visitors and museums together so they work in harmony, each being fulfilled through a shared experience with the other.

Everything that a museum provides its visitors can be considered as a starting 'offer' that expresses the museum's motivation. Our visitor might respond by yes-and-ing one of these ideas, such as attending an exhibition for instance, which demonstrates their motivation. A participatory exhibition might then go one step further, accepting this offer by incorporating a spot for the visitor to respond to what they've experienced. But this is usually where it stops. Museums tend to not be very good at continuing the exchange of yes-and with visitors, taking on board their contributions and building on them. Museums are very good at explaining to visitors the benefit of having interacted with them, but poor at understanding the benefit of the museum having interacted with the visitor. Ed Rodley has questioned the "vogue for [museum] storytelling isn't in some way [a] reaction against learning better listening skills. Storytelling allows us to focus on the part we like: we talk, you listen."[13]

Museums are sites of human exchange, not static spaces. Museums will evolve through understanding why two-way interaction with visitors benefits organizations. The bond between museum and visitor can be built if this relationship is reframed as being reciprocal, and working practices are implemented that allow staff to achieve it. Museum growth, in the form of visitor engagement and impact, can be realised if this symbiotic relationship is embraced.

The performative museum is a new understanding of the museum as a site that evolves through the active and ongoing exchange of interactions with visitors. Strategically, this is a shift from the social role of the museum as a trusted and authoritative source of information that works towards education as an outcome. If instead museums work towards belonging and identity-work as a shared outcome with visitors, they need to be intentional and clearly articulate their behavioural norms to achieve an intuitive visitor experience. Without clearly articulated intention, spaces will be performative, but in ways that might feel alienating or confusing to visitors. Within this, performative museums can leverage the unique 'choose your own experience' aspect of their organization by responding to the motivations behind their visitor responses. By understand the theory outlined in this paper, which underpins the complex system that is the visitor-centered museum, staff at all levels can work together to bring the performative museum to life.

NOTES

1. Kylie Budge and Alli Burness, "Museum objects and Instagram: agency and communication in digital engagement," *Continuum*, volume 32, no 2 (2018): 137 – 150 *and* Maria Paula Arias, "Instagram Trends: Visual Narratives of Embodied Experiences at the Museum of Islamic Art," *Museums and the Web 2018*, https://mw18.mwconf.org/paper/instagram-trends-visual-narratives-of-embodied-experiences-at-the-museum-of-islamic-art/ (accessed February 9, 2019).

2. Alli Burness, Megan Estep, Jennifer Kidd, and Chad Weinard, "Putting People in the Picture: Learning from Museum Visitor Social Photos," Conference Presentation, *Museum Computer Network,* New Orleans, LA, https://youtu.be/IQ9Yvpxph8Q (accessed February 9. 2019).

3. Sophie Haigney, "The Museums of Instagram," *The New Yorker*, September 16, 2018, https://www.newyorker.com/culture/culture-desk/the-museums-of-instagram (accessed February 9 2019).

4. Judith Butler, *Gender Trouble* (New York: Routledge, 1999), xv.

5. Chris Flink quoted in Scott Doorley and Scott Witthoft, *Make Space: How to Set the Stage for Creative Collaboration* (Hoboken, NJ: John Wiley & Sons, 2012), 38-52.

6. Jay Rounds, "Doing Identity Work in Museum," *Curator: The Museum Journal*, Volume 49, Issue 2, April 2006, 133 - 150, 133.

7. Kingsley Jayasekera, "China Unlimited: Understanding the Museum Boom in China,"

Communicating the Museum, 2014, https://www.youtube.com/
watch?time_continue=106&v=ZV_bWc1OA5c (accessed February 9, 2019).

8. Alli Burness, "New Ways of Looking: Self-representational social photography in museums," *Museums and Visitor Photography: Redefining the Visitor Experience*, edited by Theopisti Stylianou-Lambert, 90 - 127. Museums Etc, 2016.

9. Richard Holledge, "Down with Blockbusters! James Bradburne on the art of running a museum," *Financial Times*, January 22, 2018, https://www.ft.com/content/dc3e411c-f20b-11e7-bb7d-c3edfe974e9f (accessed February 9, 2019).

10. Kees Dorst, *Frame Innovation: Create New Thinking By Design* (Boston, Ma: MIT Press, 2015), 45 - 53.

11. For example, an improv scene might progress like this:

    "We're sisters"

    "Yes, and we've inherited our mother's business"

    "Yes, and she was an assassin."

    "Yes, and we need to avenge her murder!"

12. John Falk, *Identity and the Museum Visitor Experience* (Walnut Creek, CA: Left Coast Press, 2019), and Morris Hargreaves Mcintyre, *Culture Segments*, https://mhminsight.com/culture-segments (accessed February 10, 2019).

13. Ed Rodley, Twitter Post, June 23, 2017, 10.40pm, https://twitter.com/erodley/status/878231357813665792 (accessed February 9, 2019).

BIBLIOGRAPHY

Arias, Maria Paula. "Instagram Trends: Visual Narratives of Embodied Experiences at the Museum of Islamic Art." *Museums and the Web 2018*, January 14, 2018. https://mw18.mwconf.org/paper/instagram-trends-visual-narratives-of-embodied-experiences-at-the-museum-of-islamic-art/ (associated February 9, 2019).

Budge, Kylie, and Alli Burness. "Museum objects and Instagram: agency and communication in digital engagement." *Continuum*, volume 32, no 2 (2018): 137 - 150.

Burness, Alli. "New Ways of Looking: Self-representational social photography in museums." *Museums and Visitor Photography: Redefining the Visitor Experience*, edited by Theopisti Stylianou-Lambert, 90 - 127. Museums Etc, 2016.

Burness, Alli, Megan Estep, Jennifer Kidd, and Chad Weinard. "Putting People in the Picture: Learning from Museum Visitor Social Photos." Conference Presentation. *Museum Computer Network*, New Orleans, LA, 2016. https://youtu.be/IQ9Yvpxph8Q (accessed February 9, 2019).

Butler, Judith. *Gender Trouble*. New York: Routledge, 1999.

Doorley, Scott, and Scott Witthoft. *Make Space: How to Set the Stage for Creative Collaboration*. Hoboken, NJ: John Wiley & Sons, 2012.

Dorst, Kees. *Frame Innovation: Create New Thinking By Design*. Boston, MA: MIT Press, 2015.

Falk, John. *Identity and the Museum Visitor Experience*. Walnut Creek, CA: Left Coast Press, 2019.

Haigney, Sophie. "The Museums of Instagram." *The New Yorker*, September 16, 2018. https://www.newyorker.com/culture/culture-desk/the-museums-of-instagram (accessed February 9, 2019).

Holledge, Richard. "Down with Blockbusters! James Bradburne on the art of running a museum." *Financial Times*, January 22, 2018. https://www.ft.com/content/dc3e411c-f20b-11e7-bb7d-c3edfe974e9f (accessed February 9, 2019).

Jayasekera, Kingsley. "China Unlimited: Understanding the Museum Boom in China." *Communicating the Museum*, 2014. https://www.youtube.com/watch?time_continue=106&v=ZV_bWc1OA5c (assessed February 9, 2019).

Mcintyre, Morris Hargreaves. *Culture Segments*. https://mhminsight.com/culture-segments (accessed February 10, 2019).

Rodley, Ed. Twitter Post. June 23, 2017, 10:40pm. https://twitter.com/erodley/status/878231357813665792 (accessed February 9, 2019).

Rounds, Jay. "Doing Identity Work in Museums." *Curator: The Museum Journal*, Volume 49, Issue 2, April 2006, 133 - 150.

Chapter 8

Abandon Your Recipes: Three Keys to Building Experience Sessions and Why You Should Try It

Rachel Ropeik

The room you've just walked into is dark, curtains drawn, dimly lit at one end by fairy lights strung around the walls and ceiling. The air is scented with bundles of dried herbs. An altar table at the center radiates with the warm, flickering glow of candlelight. You're invited to sit comfortably on upholstered chairs or the floor, in small circles of like-minded friends and soon-to-be friends. Breathe. A bell chimes resonantly and someone murmurs, low and intimate, through an earbud in your ear: Removing or changing almost any inequity will require persistent, long-term effort. *Your group of friends mulls this idea over in quiet conversation until the bell chimes again, and the voice in your ear comes back with more words to ponder. You discuss, hear more words in your ear, and discuss again. Eventually, your departure from the room is accompanied by music playing and a parting invitation to keep wondering.*

For most people, what I have described above is not the typical experience of a professional conference session. Nevertheless, this was a session I led at the 2017 Museum Computer Network conference. It was called Slow Change: It's Not a Consolation Prize,[1] and it was an example of what I have come to call Experience Sessions: museum programs, conference sessions, and training workshops that focus as much on the quality and mood of the group's time together as the content covered; that devote care and attention to the HOW of the session as much as the WHAT.

Experience Sessions are something I began offering years ago when I swore to myself that I'd never again give a conference presentation that followed the standard "PowerPoint slides + Q&A" format. I learn best about the interesting work people have done by seeing examples of it. When I leave the conference fog of several days' intense mental focus, what I remember are the moments that broke the pattern and asked me to be in a different way. So those are the sessions I aim to create for others. In the past few years, I've seen a rise in Experience Sessions, and since I work full-time making museum experiences, I want to share some of the ideas underpinning good ones. How might you go about making your own Experience Session? Why bother with it in the first place? Gather round, as the storyteller might say, and come with me as I offer some suggestions.

✦   ✦   ✦

You've arrived at the museum on a Tuesday evening after work. You're here on a second date, and things are a little stiff. The air conditioning is a refreshing change from the humid summer air outside. As you walk through galleries of sculptures and paintings, a museum staffer approaches you. She asks you, somewhat mysteriously, to participate in an exchange she's running in the museum that night. You're not sure you want to, but your date seems cautiously intrigued. What kind of exchange? they ask, and the staffer tells you it's an exchange of words. She asks you and your date to give her three separate words about your time in the museum that day, which she writes neatly on three separate cards with the museum's logo at the bottom. She reminds you that an exchange goes both ways and offers you words that other museum visitors have given her that evening by reaching into her pocket for a stack of cards. She gives

you and your date each a card with a single word written on it: EVOCATIVE.
FROLIC. Your card has a nice weight to it. It feels good in your hand. The staffer
suggests that you can allow your words to influence the rest of your visit as
much or as little as you like and that the cards are yours to keep before she
thanks you and wanders off into the galleries.

Reading that description of a recent Gallery Encounter I created in the museum where I work[2] (an in-museum version of an Experience Session), you might be reacting in any number of ways. That might sound right up your alley. It might sound awkward and invasive. It may or may not be the kind of thing you'd like to participate in yourself. Which brings me to my first key to creating a good Experience Session. **An Experience Session Won't Be for Everyone**. The sooner you can embrace that knowledge, the sooner you'll be able to commit to creating a truly memorable encounter. Priya Parker—whose book, *The Art of Gathering*, is indispensable reading for anyone interested in making Experience Sessions—sums up the philosophy behind this. "Gatherings that are willing to be alienating—which is different from being alienating—have a better chance to dazzle."[3] You have to risk leaving some people unimpressed for someone else to be really wowed.

In the Slow Change conference session, I asked participants to stay in the room and be attentive and present for the entire window of time. I asked them to be open (and vulnerable) to new ideas that might push at their own behavioral norms or workplace expectations. Those are big asks and not ones everyone at a professional conference wants to answer. When I approached people to participate in the Gallery Encounter, some weren't interested. That was fine. I moved on to speak with someone else. Part of what makes an Experience Session truly connect is that it centers the people who opt-in. It's their experience. I'm framing that experience, yes, but it's not really about me and my priorities. To make it happen well, I need to set up the framework and guide the participants, but I must be willing to give up some of my own authority during our shared time, to let go of knowing exactly what will happen and allow the participants to make what they want of their time.

That's the second key: **De-Center Yourself, Give up Control, and Let It Be**. I know this is hard, and it may seem counterintuitive. You have wisdom to share, and people are coming to you to hear it. You have a limited amount of time that you don't want to waste. Those things are worth keeping in mind, yes, but if they are the most important motivators behind what you're doing, then an Experience Session is not what you're after. If what you are truly committed to is an Experience Session, then you are not only focusing on a topic, but aiming to bring a particular atmosphere and mood to your gathering. You're approaching your gathering like Claude Monet, who set out to make his painting subjects not just haystacks and cathedrals and water lilies, but "the envelope" of weather and light and aura that surrounded those things. How you want to build your chosen aura will begin with your own inspiration, but it must then leave room for what others bring with them, and you must be okay with that being outside your own control.

✦　　✦　　✦

You've come to this museum for the first time and with only a sketchy idea of what you're about to do this evening. While you do have a background in leading experiences with museum objects you're familiar with, tonight you've arrived to participate in an event with a collection you don't know. You're randomly assigned an object on view, and randomly assigned two collaborators to work with who have come with the same mix of trepidation and excitement you're feeling yourself. The brief for your trio: you have 45 minutes to develop a six-minute experience that engages people with your assigned object. No more detail is given, only an encouragement to keep an open mind and a supportive spirit throughout the evening and to be okay trying things that scare you. You don't have your usual planning time or research resources at hand. You've got to work with a couple of strangers and then conduct your experience for a group of 30 more. Your 45 minutes of preparation speed by, without enough time to second-guess yourself, and then you're tossed into a quick progression through leading your experience and participating in another half-dozen, created by your colleagues with other objects around the galleries. Some are lively, some solemn. You write and dance and laugh and think and talk to strangers and invent sounds. It is an evening full of surprises, and you leave with new ideas and new energy.

This was the first Museum Teaching Mashup,[4] which I co-facilitated in 2015 at the Ogden Museum of Southern Art in New Orleans. It was held during the museum's weeknight evening hours after a day of the National Art Education Association annual conference, and, in contrast to the formal presentations that art educators had been leading and listening to throughout the day, this event was set up to intentionally make space for not knowing what would happen. Everyone there had to trust their collaborators and the larger group, and no one could make anything go completely to plan. It was a capital-E-S Experience Session, and I share here one participant's reflection (solicited in writing after a week had passed) that illustrates what can happen when people give up their comfortable control.

[I]t was particularly challenging to adapt as people responded to our instructions in a different way than I expected. We purposefully kept the instructions minimal

but I had a specific behavior in mind. When that didn't happen I momentarily panicked but decided to go with it instead of redirect people and see what happened. It wasn't what we envisioned but I liked what happened...upon reflection, I see how important it is to let the people you work with and collaborate with feel empowered to contribute their ideas (even unrehearsed) and innovate. When we shut voices down or make every moment be carefully scripted, we may lose a spectacular idea.

In talking about this, I often use the metaphor of reins. There will be moments where you as facilitator need to hold the reins more tightly, but think of those as the framing moments rather than the bulk of your time, the bread of the sandwich rather than the meat. To take the example of the Museum Teaching Mashup, my co-facilitator and I opened with exercises to get energy flowing and promote a spirit of supportive creativity, and we closed with expressive gratitude and collective congratulations for everyone's willing hearts and clever minds. During the bulk of the evening, however, we were there merely as timekeepers, while our participants literally led the show.

I want to offer an important, cautioning caveat here. De-centering yourself and letting others have control does not absolve you of all responsibility. You need to know when to pick up the reins. If, for example, during your Experience Session, someone says or does something offensive or hurtful, it's up to you to step in and address the situation. If someone's participation is taking your Experience Session beyond the scope of what you are there for (we've all heard the person who blithely diverts or dominates the cocktail party conversation), it's up to you to steer things back on track. Pick up the reins when you need to. But then be able to loosen your grip on them again.

By giving up this control, you may be making yourself less comfortable, but remember that you're de-centering yourself here. Instead, you are giving a gift to the participants in your Experience Session. You are letting them make of it whatever they want it to be. You're allowing them to pass their time with you in a way that can inspire them however they are open to receive inspiration. As another Museum Teaching Mashup participant put it: *When you participate in an experience like this... you get to leave with YOUR own experience, and not the thoughts of someone else. You made meaning for yourself, and that experience is likely to continue to stay in your mind even after you leave.*

✦　　✦　　✦

You've responded to a tweet from someone you know only vaguely about proposing a conference session around how digital technology can help or hinder empathy building. It's something that's been on your mind recently both in and out of your office. You trade some emails back and forth with the others who also responded to this tweet, set up a time for an initial video call, and proceed through several months of idea generation sparked by five creative brains suggesting things thoughtfully, attentively, kindly, and without prematurely shutting down avenues of exploration. Your conference session planning itself becomes a creative process that leads you to new references, pulls in some of your own favorite sources of inspiration, and builds tools that will be useful in your daily work.

In this final scenario, you are me. It's something of a meta-reflection on the experience of creating an Experience Session, in this case, the Empathy Jam[5] session at MCN 2018. We've written about that collaboration at the end of this book, but it absolutely typified my third and final key to successfully putting together an Experience Session: **Plan and Proceed with Curiosity and Collaboration**.

It's hard to plan Experience Sessions alone. It's hard to give up control or develop a deeply impactful, potentially alienating Experience Session without the power of multiple minds at work. In all the examples I've included here, I planned in collaboration with others and depended on their feedback to make changes as I went. If it's a conference session, join forces with like-minded peers. If it's a project at work, enlist colleagues to test beta versions of your plan. If you really do want to make room for an encounter that feels surprising and new, think about other moments when you've felt that way yourself and what conditions made it happen.

In the language of job interviews, people toss around the phrase "transferable skills." In the realm of Experience Sessions, I encourage you to apply the correlative idea of "transferable inspiration." Who and where else can you turn for the ideas that make you tingle with creative excitement? Me, I like immersive theater and motivational[6] decks[7] of cards.[8] You've surely had memorable encounters that sparked something emotionally powerful in you. Think about what elements of those Experience Sessions designed by others you might adapt to suit the purpose of your own.

To recap, here are three foundational keys for building Experience Sessions:

- ✦ **An Experience Session Won't Be for Everyone**
- ✦ **De-Center Yourself, Give up Control, and Let It Be**
- ✦ **Plan and Proceed with Curiosity and Collaboration**

I highly encourage you to fill out your keyring with your own additional keys. And I highly encourage you to consider taking the risk of developing Experience Sessions in the first place. They are certainly more challenging to create than a "PowerPoint slides + Q&A" presentation, but just as certainly more memorable and rewarding for you and the participants who decide to dive into the pool with you. So the next time you see a call for conference proposals or have a meeting to run or a workshop to plan, think about creating an Experience Session instead of your go-to, well-trod format. To borrow a randomly selected, perfectly apt Oblique Strategies prompt: *Discover the recipes you are using and abandon them.*

NOTES

1. "Slow Change: It's Not a Consolation Prize," Conference Presentation, *Museum Computer Network*, Pittsburgh, PA, 2017. https://bit.ly/2tojJP0 (accessed February 17, 2019).

2. Rachel Ropeik, "There's No Right Way to Visit a Museum: Creating a New Summer Experience at the Guggenheim," *Checklist*, July 25, 2018, https://bit.ly/2NbGTkN (accessed February 17, 2019).

3. Priya Parker, *The Art of Gathering: How We Meet and Why It Matters* (New York: Riverhead Books, 2018), 23.

4. Rachel Ropeik, "Reflections on a Museum Experiment: Thoughts About the Museum Teaching Mashup," *Medium,* April 13, 2015, https://bit.ly/2V7lvQz (accessed February 17, 2019).

5. "Empathy Jam," Conference Presentation, *Museum Computer Network,* Denver, CO, 2018, https://bit.ly/2SQcPk7 (accessed February 17, 2019).

6. Katya Tylevich and Mikkel Sommer Christensen, *Art Oracles: Creative & Life Inspiration from the Great Artists*, Card deck, (London: Laurence King Publishing Ltd., August 7, 2017).

7. "The Space Deck,' *MuseumCamp*. Card deck, 2015.

8. Brian Eno and Peter Schmidt, "Oblique Strategies," *Oblique Strategies*, http://obliquestrategies.ca/ (accessed February 17, 2019).

BIBLIOGRAPHY

"Empathy Jam." Conference Presentation. *Museum Computer Network*, Denver, CO, 2018. https://bit.ly/2SQcPk7 (accessed February 17, 2019).

Eno, Brian, and Peter Schmidt. "Oblique Strategies." *Oblique Strategies*. http://obliquestrategies.ca/ (accessed March 03, 2019).

Parker, Priya. *The Art of Gathering: How We Meet and Why It Matters*. New York: Riverhead Books, 2018.

Ropeik, Rachel. "Reflections on a Museum Experiment: Thoughts About the Museum Teaching Mashup." *Medium*. April 13, 2015. https://bit.ly/2V7lvQz (accessed February 17, 2019).

———. "There's No Right Way to Visit a Museum: Creating a New Summer Experience at the Guggenheim." *Checklist*. July 25, 2018. https://bit.ly/2NbGTkN (accessed February 17, 2019).

"Slow Change: It's Not a Consolation Prize," Conference Presentation, *Museum Computer Network*, Pittsburgh, PA, 2017. https://bit.ly/2tojJP0 (accessed February 17, 2019).

"The Space Deck," *MuseumCamp*. Card deck, 2015.

Tylevich, Katya, and Mikkel Sommer Christensen. *Art Oracles: Creative & Life Inspiration from the Great Artists*. Card deck. London: Laurence King Publishing Ltd., August 7, 2017.

Chapter 9

Talking Inclusion with the 2018 MCN Scholars

Jessica BrodeFrank

The future of museums is inclusion and diversity. These two buzzwords are in almost every museum's mission, values, or brand statement; but how are we outwardly reflecting it in outdated exhibits and Eurocentric narratives? The digital space is an opportunity to be more intersectional. As stated in the *Digital Humanities Quarterly*, the digital space has become the forefront for interactions with the humanities:

> *The humanities have become digital by making the objects of study available in digital form, by introducing digital analytical tools, and by establishing digital means of communication for collaborating during the research process, for discussing and disseminating research results and for interacting with society at large.*[1]

The MCN Scholars Program[2] represents 15 emerging museum professionals from various cultural heritage sectors and the work they're doing to innovate the museum world, specifically in the digital realm. This year we saw Twitter mascots, museum memes, MOOCs, and online exclusive museums. Overarching across many of the scholars' presentations was the role technology can play in bringing diversity to our institutional messaging. Of the 14 scholars who spoke, three in particular made specific case studies of this kind of inclusive narrative online and I will cover that here: Shaz Hussain of the Science Museum London, Isabel Brador of the Wolfsonian-FIU, and Ravon Ruffin of the National Museum of African American History and Culture (NMAAHC).

Museum Detox

Shaz Hussain of the Science Museum London also works as a pioneering member of the group Museum Detox. Her presentation at the 2018 MCN Conference focused on the work done as a part of Museum Detox, specifically the White Privilege Clinic. As stated on their own website, Museum Detox:

> is a network of people from diverse ethnic backgrounds who creatively use radical approaches to dismantle unjust infrastructures in our national cultural institutions. We start by challenging our own conscious biases, prejudices and stereotypes that we hold on ourselves and others. Through open and honest conversations, and surveys with our growing membership base, we share our views and concerns with the sector we work in.[3]

This sector, the museum sector, has a problem with diversity. According to Mariet Westermann, executive vice president of the Andrew W. Mellon Foundation, "the situation was worse than in almost any sector I've seen."[4]

Westermann was referencing the issue of representation within museum staffs. A national study conducted in 2015 by the Mellon Foundation found that in art museums only 16 percent of leadership positions are held by people of color, although 38 percent of Americans identify as non-Caucasian.[5]

To address such a disproportionate representation within museum staffing, Museum Detox brought forward the White Privilege Clinic. This was presented at the Museums Association Conference in Manchester, UK. It challenged conference-goers to take a test to check their white privilege with Museum Detox staff acting as "doctors" who went over their "patients'" test results and gave "prescriptions" to address these biases. As Hussain stated after the experiment:

> I invited you to take the test because I wanted you to put yourself in the shoes of a person of colour. To see the other side of the same coin. I look you dead in the eyes and tell you my lived experience of racism. I ask you what you are going to do, with whatever amount of privilege you have, to help in this fight. Your white privilege is such an empowering thing. I believe that you can make change.[6]

The White Privilege Clinic won "best product" at the conference, and more than that, inspired Twitter discussions where "patients" shared how they would remedy their own white privilege, allowing a safe space to begin these difficult but necessary conversations. We cannot hope to diversify our narratives until we first recognize the biases we present to our public every single day, and this is what the Museum Detox group is advocating for.

Metadata Squad

One way museums can truly begin to face their white privilege might reside in creating better-researched metadata to uncover stories we never thought to look for within our White Eurocentric narratives. Metadata is the unsexy cousin of digital initiatives. It's not something donors are lining up to fund but without it how can we expect to do anything else. When a social media specialist asks for what you can post for a specific theme, you need to be able to search your database for terms that will bring up correlating material; without metadata this search is useless. Prominent digital humanists like Lev Manovich have long argued that "objects remain effectively invisible without adequate database search functionality."[7] Yet if we don't have the time and we don't have funding to do proper metadata tagging how can we get it done?

This was a question that the Wolfsonian-FIU faced. The Metadata Squad was created to do this essential but often-overlooked task, bringing on a team of graduate students who are paid to dig deep into the metadata for objects that either have yet to be verified or have yet to be researched. Isabel Brador spoke on the creation of the Metadata Squad as a reciprocal learning experience; graduate students learning valuable research skills, and the Wolfsonian learning more about their collection.

The information gathered by the Metadata Squad has allowed the Wolfsonian to discover and tell more representative stories. Brador spoke of one example of the ceramicist Edris Eckhardt whose works are housed in the Wolfsonian. One of the members in the Metadata Squad added to the Wolfsonian metadata to include the story of how Edris Eckhardt changed her name from Edith to Edris to sound more androgynous after losing commissions to male counterparts.[8]

With proper metadata it becomes much easier to find objects that have unique, diverse, and inclusive stories outside the typical narrative. As stated by Kate Holterhoff in the *Digital Humanities Quarterly*, "I contend that improving database search functionality through heavy editing-metadata is voluminous, polyvocal, and critical... is at present the best means for facilitating digital image archives to contribute increasingly significant socio-political projects."[9] These deep dives done by institutions like the Wolfsonian are great to start internally, but useless if not shared externally with the public. One of the easiest, cheapest, and widest-ranging ways to share this kind of content is through social media.

#trending on Social

Despite the rise in popularity of social media platforms within the everyday person's daily life "in the museum digital field, a lot of museums don't invest in social," says Lanae Spruce, Manager of Social Media (NMAAHC).[10] Spruce and Ravon Ruffin lead the National Museum of African American History and Culture's social media presence, and from day one the museum has noted the need for investment in social. Part of the museum's mission is to fuse African American history into every day thought and life. Through social media, NMAAHC is able to continually contribute threads to popular conversation.

In March, Spruce and Ruffin started a thread on Twitter with the hashtag #hiddenherstory to honor Women's History Month. Every day, they shared facts about black women to "celebrate the legacy of women who were often unsung in traditional historical narratives."[11] The hashtag took off, and audiences reveled in the stories the team told with only 140 characters and an image. From Claudette Colvin, a 15-year-old girl who refused to give up her seat on a segregated Montgomery bus prior to Rosa Parks, to Bridget "Biddy" Mason, a formerly enslaved woman who sued for her freedom and became one of the first black women to own land in California, "people don't know these stories," Spruce said.[12] On social, people thanked NMAAHC for sharing and even asked for more. They saw women who, despite dealing with segregation and gender discrimination, "were empowering during a time when so many people tried to stifle black women."[13]

Similarly, #blackmensmiling began trending in 2018, and NMAAHC joined this already-trending hashtag with their museum content. Twitter credits comedian Dennis Banks for starting the hashtag on February 2, 2018 and as it trended for much of that day and the next, NMAAHC joined in the conversation. Shortly after, many celebrities and other institutions joined and threaded with them on Twitter.[14]

NMAAHC has provided a space where people can go, not only to engage and tell their own stories but to see diverse stories told. This is the power social media holds.

Conclusion

As the MCN Scholars program looks at the future of museum professionals, the MCN Scholars themselves are showing that the future of museums is more diverse and inclusive. As museums begin to confront their own biases, discover their own diverse stories, and share these stories with the world, we will hopefully begin to see museums transitioning to the inclusive spaces we've always wished them to be.

NOTES

1. Niels Brugger, "Digital Humanities in the 21st Century: Digital Material as a Driving Force," *Digital Humanities Quarterly,* Volume 10, no. 2 (2016).

2. "2018 Scholars," Conference presentation, *Museum Computer Network,* Denver, CO, 2018. http://conference.mcn.edu/2018/scholars.cfm (accessed January 18, 2019).

3. "Meet Our Team," *Museum Detox,* http://museumdetox.com/#team-5 (accessed January 18, 2019).

4. Robin Pogrebin, "With New Urgency, Museums Cultivate Creators of Color," *New York Times,* August 8, 2018, https://www.nytimes.com/2018/08/08/arts/design/museums-curators-diversity-employment.html (accessed February 8, 2019).

5. Pogrebin, 2018.

6. Shaz Hussain."The White Privilege Clinic | An Open Letter to my white colleagues," *Medium,* February 20, 2018, https://medium.com/mcnx-london/the-white-privilege-clinic-an-open-letter-to-my-white-colleagues-d336e0a4206d (accessed February 8, 2019).

7. Kate Holterhoff, "From Disclaimer to Critique: Race and the Digital Image Archivist," *Digital Humanities Quarterly,* Volume 11, no. 3 (2017).

8. "Edris Eckhardt, Pioneer in Glass Sculpture, 1905-1998," *Cleveland Arts Prize,* http://www.clevelandartsprize.org/awardees/Edris_Eckhardt.html (accessed January 25, 2019).

9. Holterhoff, 2017.

10. Ashley Nguyen, "These Two Women are Building an African American History Museum Online," *The Lily,* https://www.thelily.com/these-two-women-are-building-an-african-american-history-museum-online/ (accessed January 16, 2019).

11. Nguyen, *The Lily.*

12. Ibid.

13. Ibid.

14. Vanessa Williams, "#BlackMenSmiling: Why a small gesture caused a big reaction on Twitter," *The Washington Post,* February 3, 2018, https://www.washingtonpost.com/news/post-nation/wp/2018/02/03/blackmensmiling-why-a-small-gesture-caused-a-big-reaction-twitter/?noredirect=on&utm_term=.7f6a2125ca04 (accessed January 17, 2019).

BIBLIOGRAPHY

"2018 Scholars." Conference Proposal. *Museum Computer Network*, Denver, CO, 2018. http://conference.mcn.edu/2018/scholars.cfm (accessed January 18, 2019).

"Edris Eckhardt, Pioneer in Glass Sculpture, 1905-1998." *Cleveland Arts Prize.* http://www.clevelandartsprize.org/awardees/Edris_Eckhardt.html (accessed January 25, 2019).

"Meet Our Team." *Museum Detox.* http://museumdetox.com/#team-5 (accessed January 25, 2019).

Brügger, Niels. "Digital Humanities in the 21st Century: Digital Material as a Driving Force." *Digital Humanities Quarterly* 10, no. 2 (2016). http://digitalhumanities.org/dhq/vol/10/3/000256/000256.html (accessed January 25, 2019).

Holteroff, Kate. "From Disclaimer to Critique: Race and the Digital Image Archivist." *Digital Humanities Quarterly* 11, no. 3 (2017). http://www.digitalhumanities.org/dhq/vol/11/3/000324/000324.html.

Hussain, Shaz. "The White Privilege Clinic | An Open Letter to My White Colleagues." Medium. February 20, 2018. https://medium.com/mcnx-london/the-white-privilege-clinic-an-open-letter-to-my-white-colleagues-d336e0a4206d (accessed January 25, 2019).

Nguyen, Ashley. "These Two Women Are Building an African American History Museum." *The Lily.* August 1, 2018. https://www.thelily.com/these-two-women-are-building-an-african-american-history-museum-online/ (accessed January 25, 2019).

Pogrebin, Robin. "With New Urgency, Museums Cultivate Creators of Color." *The New York Times*, August 8, 2018. https://www.nytimes.com/2018/08/08/arts/design/museums-curators-diversity-employment.html (accessed January 25, 2019).

Williams, Vanessa. "#BlackMenSmiling: Why a Small Gesture Caused a Big Reaction on Twitter." *The Washington Post*, February 3, 2018. https://www.washingtonpost.com/news/post-nation/wp/2018/02/03/blackmensmiling-why-a-small-gesture-caused-a-big-reaction-twitter (accessed January 25, 2019).

Chapter 10

Closer Than They Appear: Drawing Lessons from Development Processes for Museum Technology, Exhibitions, and Theatrical Productions

Max Evjen
David McKenzie

Introduction

This chapter is an outgrowth of two presentations given at Museum Computer Network 2018.

Max Evjen's Ignite talk "Jazz Hands Out!: Why #Musetech Should Be Like Theatre"[1] argued that we in museum technology should reject the fail fast mentality borrowed from software firms, but rather look to theatre as a model for taking projects slowly while still iterating based on audience feedback during development. David

McKenzie's session on prototyping sprints examined the promises and limitations of a tech-firm-derived fail-fast process for creating museum exhibition components.

Unlike technology companies, museums don't have venture capitalists pouring millions into organizations so they can continually "break things and see what happens." Yet, many of us in the museum field face pressures—sometimes from ourselves—to adopt this fast-fail mentality from the tech world for our own technology projects and even for creating exhibitions. A fast-fail mentality does have the advantage of trying many ideas and learning from failure and iteration. Yet, such processes are unrealistic and, we argue, undesirable for the museum world beyond certain limited uses. For many reasons, production processes in the museum world—both for exhibitions and even for technology—follow a waterfall format and require a great deal more deliberation. Rather than rejecting this model in favor of the fast-fail model of technology companies, we argue that museum professionals should look to another, more-adjacent field, theatrical production, for how to bring more iteration and audience responsiveness into our projects while not losing the virtues of our longer, deliberative production processes. At the same time, we also argue that theatre professionals can learn from museum professionals in incorporating more continual feedback throughout the production process.

In this piece, we first discuss a tech-firm-derived process—prototyping sprints—that Ford's Theatre used with success, up to a point. Then we discuss how museums can learn from theatrical production processes for development of both exhibitions and museum technology, while comparing and critiquing all three processes and suggesting practices that each can borrow from the other(s), rather than scuttling our processes in favor of the latest from Silicon Valley. The primary focus of critique will be on how we can better create end products around the needs of constituents by involving them in the process, while not losing strengths found in each process. We also compare stages of creating theatrical productions, museum exhibitions, and museum technology.

Limitations of Fast-Fail Sprinting: An Experiment at Ford's Theatre

In recent years, museum professionals have borrowed some fast-fail techniques from the technology world, with some limited but helpful applicability. Prototyping sprints are one such technique. In late 2017 and early 2018, McKenzie and his colleagues at Ford's Theatre embarked on a series of six week-long prototyping sprints to find ways to engage students in the site's encyclopedic, text-heavy core exhibition. Ford's Theatre used a five-day sprint process that began with an ideation session on day 1 that produced—ending with an agreement on an idea to test. Days 2 and 3 involved building the prototype. Day 4 included testing of the prototype on the floor, with a debrief on the fifth day. This technique has found some use in museum spaces, most notably by Shelley Bernstein and Sarah Devine at the Brooklyn Museum and by Bernstein at the Barnes Collection.[2]

Evaluator and facilitator Kate Haley Goldman, following the direction set by Ford's Director of Education and Interpretation Sarah Jencks, adapted the sprinting technique from methods Google and other technology companies use to find quick and dirty solutions to specific problems.[3]

This experience demonstrated promises and pitfalls of a tech-firm-derived fail-fast paradigm. While it proved overall worthwhile—it was helpful for learning quickly about ideas that may or may not work and, as a side benefit, increased staff cohesion—it did not work for developing an idea beyond initial concept stage. During the six designated sprint weeks, Ford's Theatre staff members were able to try and discard ideas that, in many cases, had been discussed but not acted upon for years.

This process also yielded an end product that Ford's Theatre could use—a set of historical figure cards and flip doors to help students connect with individuals from the era interpreted. After finding success with this idea during the fourth sprint week, the team created and quickly tested new iterations during the fifth and sixth weeks. This was when the limited applicability of the process became clear. There was only so much iteration that could take place in a short time frame. Actual design, development, and installation is following a more traditional waterfall process, more akin to exhibition and theatre production. However, because of the experience, Ford's staff is also wary of building permanently printed flip doors. Instead, the end product will be a set of flip doors with windows, allowing for continual evaluation of content and resultant iteration.

Comparison of Different Processes

So, if we want to take some of the good from fast-fail approaches—quick audience feedback—while realizing the technique's limited applicability, what are we to do? As museum professionals, one direction we can look is to theater. Before diving into what we can learn from our arts and culture world colleagues, below we share a table comparing the very basic steps in Museum Exhibition, Museum Technology, and Theatrical Production processes—realizing that these vary across institutions and projects.

Development Stages	Museum Exhibition	Museum Technology	Theatrical Production
Strategy	*Interpretive Planning:* setting messages and takeaways. May include audience feedback.	*Digital Strategy:* setting direction for digital efforts. May include audience	*Performance selection:* devising, season/show selection. May include audience feedback.
Requirements	*Concept/Schematic Design:* Preliminary design approaches, nailing down the big picture. Still room to change course. Maybe some degree of audience feedback.	*Requirements:* Assessing the technical needs, organizing digital resources, possible purchasing digital resources. Still room to change course.	*Production Meetings:* Establishing big picture design concepts. Table Read. Surround Events may include audience feedback.
Design	*Design Development:* Filling in some details, narrowing down script, still room for tweaks. Likely little or no audience feedback.	*Preliminary Design:* Paper prototyping, audience feedback is essential at this point.	*Rehearsals,* filling and narrowing down script and blocking, still room for tweaks. Likely little or no audience feedback, except in the case of commercial theatre workshops, which rely heavily on audience feedback.
Development	*Final Design:* Filling in all details, finalizing the script. Little room for tweaks except of details. Likely little or no audience feedback.	*Development:* Filling in details, finalizing script/ expression. This may include iteration of develop/ test>develop/ test.	*Tech Rehearsal:* Lining up technical aspects of production with cues in script. Little or no audience feedback. Iterative process.

Development Stages	Museum Exhibition	Museum Technology	Theatrical Production
Testing	*Production Documentation:* Translating final design documents into construction drawings. Little room for tweaks except for value engineering, practical considerations. No audience feedback.	*Testing:* Audience feedback is incorporated, final adjustments made prior to launch.	*Previews/Dress Rehearsal:* Show presented in front of audience to gauge audience interest and experience to make any final changes. Audience feedback is essential.
Implementation	*Exhibition opening:* Little room for change/some room for change.	*Implementation:* Product launch, little room for change.	*Opening:* Little room for change, only practical considerations.
Evaluation	*Summative Evaluation:* Audience feedback. Little room for tweaks; most often, large-scale changes expensive, impractical.	*Summative Evaluation:* Audience feedback. Little room for tweaks; most often, large-scale changes expensive, impractical.	*Summative Evaluation:* opportunity - not often seen as essential to Production as it is in Museum Exhibitions or Museum Technology.

Theatrical Production Models

Strategy: Theatrical production begins either with a script that is selected to be produced, a choreography that is set on a dance troupe, or a devised work that is created from some prompt (including themes, sites, or other inspirations). At this point, audiences who are familiar with a production company may be enlisted to provide feedback on what works are to be produced, but often the decision to produce a theatrical production lies with the artistic team.

Requirements: In the case of a company selecting a script to be produced, once the cast and designers have been selected, there are production meetings wherein the director meets with the designers (lights, sound, sets, costumes, projection, musical director if the production is a musical) to discuss their vision for the show. A table read is scheduled where cast, directors, designers, and stage managers sit around a table and read the script aloud. That typically denotes the beginning of rehearsals for the actors and stage managers. During this time some productions may conduct surround events to market the production by building word of mouth. These may include scene readings for special events, or previews of musical numbers. Audience feedback is gathered at events like these, and that feedback can inform the notes for the remainder of rehearsals.

Design: Rehearsals typically take place in rehearsal rooms outside of the theater in which the production will happen. In the case of commercial theatre productions, shows are not just opened, they must go through a workshop (a performance with scaled down production value [lights, sound, sets, etc.] that costs significantly less than a full production so they can test the show and get audience feedback.

Development: When the actors get in the theater it is typically after all design elements (set, lighting, sound, costumes, projections) "loaded in" to the theater. Then all the design elements are matched up with the cues from the actor's performance. This is called a technical rehearsal (during "tech week") during which actors must make repeated entries and exits, and speak specific lines from scenes so the technical elements can all be matched up into a series of sequential cues.

Testing: After the long days of tech rehearsals, there may be previews, shows before opening when adjustments can be made to the production (often based on audience feedback, in addition to Director's preference), and when critics may be invited so they can write reviews before the "opening night."

Implementation: On opening night, the responsibility for the production rests with the Stage Manager, and few, only minor, practical adjustments to the production are made during the course of a production.

Evaluation: Summative evaluation is rarely considered for theatrical production, except in the case of "post-mortems" (production meetings occurring after the show is closed to consider what worked and what did not).

Issues and Critiques of Theatrical Production Models

In the long history of theatrical production, there has always been consideration for what might be appealing to audiences, or what audiences may enjoy different types of productions.[4] However, there is not the same attention given to goals (or outcomes) as there is in exhibition development, where experience goals, learning goals, and affect goals are created in advance of the development of the exhibitions. Many times, performing arts organizations will just create a production irrespective of a specific target audience, especially beyond people who traditionally attend performing arts. Both museums' and performing arts organizations' largest visitor base are old and white. If they don't consider appealing to non-traditional audiences they both run the risk of becoming irrelevant to most people.[5][6] How might targets help productions reach non-traditional audiences? How might goals that are shown to be reached through evaluation speak to the need for funding future productions?

Exhibition Development Models

Strategy: Exhibition development ideally begins with high-level strategic planning—often, but not always, interpretive planning. This sets the direction for where the exhibitions or museum technology projects will ultimately focus, and where they will not. Often in the past, the vision for exhibitions at this stage largely came from curators. More recently, though, audience feedback—often as a formative evaluation involving focus groups and surveys—has come into the picture at this stage. Although things are changing (as discussed below), this is often the last moment where audience members are involved in creating an exhibition.

Requirements, Design, Development, and Testing: The exhibition development process—largely built upon architectural design processes—proceeds from big picture concepts to filling in the details. At each stage, designers present conceptual drawings and models to the rest of the project team. Sometimes audience members will be involved, but more often will not.

Implementation and Evaluation: By the time of opening and product launch, museum exhibitions are largely set. Even when institutions undertake summative evaluation—again, often through surveys, observations, and focus groups—changes are often small and around the edges, rather than major, even if major issues are discovered. Unless an institution puts significant money into the budget for post-opening changes, more often, audience feedback is chalked up to lessons learned for future projects.

Museum Technology Model

Strategy: Similar to an exhibition, often the initial idea for a museum technology product comes from internal staff; quite often, museum technology projects are supplements to exhibitions. There may be audience feedback in conceptualizing an idea, but the concept itself is often driven by institutional objectives.

Requirements, Design, Development, Testing: Like with exhibition design, these stages involve filling in the details of the project. Museum technology projects involve considerable iteration at later stages, in part due to the nature of digital technology—where a minimum viable product can be built, then added onto—whereas exhibition projects, due to the need to have every detail in place before the exhibition can be built, become less iterative at later stages. In other words, there is no minimum viable product for a building, and it is difficult to find a similar analogy for an exhibition.[7] As this process proceeds, unlike what happens with exhibitions, audience members often get more involved in testing functionality, although not always the content or messaging—particularly before launch. For example, web testing often involves asking potential users to complete a task, rather than gauge their interest in the content of the website.

Implementation and Evaluation: In theory, unlike with an exhibition, a museum technology product is changeable after launch. Yet, often, wholesale changes are near impossible, as the infrastructure is set. Evaluation often shows tweaks that can be made. Often, if a museum technology product fails, the museum is left with little choice but to decide between continuing to maintain it or declare it a failure and sunset it—something museums are often loathe to do.

Issues and Critiques of Exhibition Development and Museum Technology Development Models

Both of these models have generally served museums well. They reflect the deliberative nature of many institutions—entities that cannot simply break things and keep trying. They result in vetted, accurate, trustworthy end products that reflect and reinforce the trust that survey after survey shows the U.S. public places in museums. An experience with deep, thoughtful content requires time to develop, like a theatrical production does. These processes, finely developed over time, suit their institutions well and, we argue, require tweaking rather than wholesale change.

What Different Models Can Learn From One Other

The main tweak we suggest involves audience feedback and continual iteration, often missing from exhibition development and even some museum technology processes. This has, all too often, resulted in exhibitions and technology products that receive rave reviews from fellow experts and fail to engage their target audiences. Yet, we are often then stuck with the results for years, if not decades. Unlike a theatrical production, an exhibition that fails to engage its audiences often nonetheless is not closed. How can we make these semi-permanent end products more responsive to audience needs and interests throughout the process? Perhaps theatre can help us with this question, while museums can also offer ideas that could improve the theatrical production process. Below we identify five prompts about each process to elaborate further on potential learnings.

Focus on entertaining the audience

In Evjen's Ignite talk he asserted that theatrical organizations understand that if audiences don't show up, a production gets cancelled. Museums don't operate with that same kind of urgency, but they should. According to Colleen Dilenschneider[8] for all arts & cultural organizations "Once adjusted for population growth, flat attendance is declining attendance." It's a safe bet that many museums would love to have the attendance numbers and press of *Hamilton (with a Broadway production in New York City, additional productions in Chicago and Puerto Rico, and a national tour.).* To be fair, many theatre companies would, too, but there is a reason that some Broadway shows have extensive runs: they provide entertaining experiences that are relevant to audiences. Museums need to remember "entertainment value motivates visitation while education value tends to justify a visit."[9]

Iteration/Waterfall models

Evjen's Ignite talk was a call to reject "fail fast" mentality and for museums to learn from theatrical production processes that iterate, just not in a sprint-like fashion. McKenzie's presentation discussed the limited applicability of design sprints in exhibition design—a lesson that could also be applied to technology projects (originally, the project began as one to create an app or mobile-friendly website for onsite use). Chad Weinard[10] states "Grant funding, fixed requirements, timelines and resources all mean that digital projects (in museums) are almost always waterfall processes" instead of agile processes.

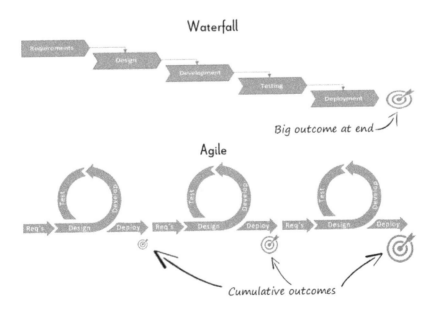

Rather than fight the waterfall process, we should embrace it, learning from theatre how to involve audiences during the process and allowing room for iteration based on feedback. After all, museums and theatres are mostly non-profit arts organizations vying for limited resources. For example, even after experimenting with prototyping, Ford's Theatre is currently exploring a more iterative and audience-informed, yet still waterfall, exhibition design process for future exhibitions.

Continual feedback

Some museums have found in recent years that there is room for audience feedback throughout exhibition design processes. Eastern State Penitentiary Historic Site in Philadelphia, for example, tested prototypes of varying levels of fidelity with on-site audiences during the entire development process for its *Prisons Today* exhibition. The exhibition team rolled out different means of showcasing specific concepts throughout the project.

Kajsa Hartig recently raised in a tweet and a Medium post the following question: what if we got audience feedback even earlier in our processes—even before we've decided whether we are doing an exhibition, public program, or event?[11] Following principles of human-centered design, she argues that we should think about designing experiences, and use audience feedback to figure out what kind of experience makes the most sense for the particular audience at the particular institution with the particular content. It may be worth exploring which audiences are invited to give feedback, as well. Different audiences have different needs and interests and will provide different kinds of feedback. Inviting in audience feedback as part of a continual feedback model, or in early decision making, makes it even more essential that museums are seeking diverse, non-binary gender specific, deliberately anti-racist, anti-ableist, representation.

Additionally, both museum technology and exhibition development processes largely get audience feedback on functionality, rather than content, as the process rolls on. What if we were testing for understanding and engagement, as well? There are some examples of movement in this area. For instance, Evjen has been working on a minimum viable product of augmented reality (AR) at the Michigan State University Museum, that included evaluation of functionality, as well as understanding and engagement. Theatrical rehearsals and previews as part of theatrical production, are inherently iterative processes that often include continual feedback during development, and commercial theatre workshops rely on audience feedback, but after a production opens consistency is the goal, except in a few special circumstances like improvisation.

Ability to tweak after launch

There is an emerging field of summative evaluation of theatrical productions, particularly in those that involve science communication.[12] Theatrical productions are constrained by the typical arrangement of the Stage Manager taking control of production upon opening. It would require new thinking to realize just how evaluation results could inform productions after opening, when the Director is no longer in control of the production, and after reviews of the production have been released. Museum exhibitions do not suffer from this particular process constraint, and museums are very accustomed to informing exhibitions at various stages including front-end evaluation, formative evaluation, remedial evaluation, and summative evaluation.[13] Perhaps theatrical organizations could learn more about how all types of evaluation could be used for the success of productions, or from museums who build in budget lines for iteration after launch.

Move from cabinets of curiosity to focus on audience experience

The performing arts have a history as ritual and immersive environments while museums carry the weight of a background filled with pillaging and plundering, and cabinets of curiosities.[14] How might museums consider a new role as that of ritual and immersive environment, without ignoring their more unattractive pasts? Following the lead of thinkers like Hartig and Andrea Jones, what does it mean for us to develop experiences incorporating artifacts, rather than exhibitions of artifacts?[15][16]

Toward a Better Model

In his Ignite talk, Evjen recommended that museum professionals reach out to theatre professionals in their communities, rather than try to imitate tech companies. Museum professionals can try and learn something about their processes that may inform better museum work from professionals who work in similar institutions, rather than following the lead of companies whose end goal is selling products. Theatre professionals may also benefit from museum processes, like setting interpretive goals, identifying target audiences, and articulating evaluation plans, and they should reach out to museum professionals in their community to find out how those can be valuable for production.

There is no silver bullet, but we argue that museums and performing arts organizations need to choose an approach that works best for their own organization. As a general rule, we argue that we shouldn't adopt tech firm fast-fail ideas wholesale and throw out the waterfall processes that museum and theatre professionals have honed over the years. Rather, we should learn from one another and, most importantly, adapt our processes to have audience members involved at all stages of the process—and be willing to iterate based on their feedback. Feedback-based iteration, borrowed from theatre, rather than fast-fail, will help push our organizations forward and make exhibitions, programs, and digital experiences more relevant to different audiences.

NOTES

1. Max Evjen, "Jazz Hands Out!: Why #Musetech Should Be Like Theatre," Ignite Talk, *Museum Computer Network Conference*, Denver, CO, 2018. https://bit.ly/2N0Mb2C (accessed February 19, 2019).

2. Shelly Bernstein, "Fighting the Three Dots of User Expectation," *BKM TECH* (blog), May 6, 2015, https://www.brooklynmuseum.org/community/blogosphere/2015/05/06/fighting-the-three-dots-of-user-expectation/ (accessed February 19, 2019); *also* Shelly, Bernstein, "Learning from Agile Fails," *BKM TECH* (blog), May 5, 2015, https://www.brooklynmuseum.org/community/blogosphere/2015/05/05/learning-from-agile-fails/ (accessed February 19, 2019); *and* Sara Devine, "Agile by Design." *BKM TECH* (blog), May 14, 2015. https://www.brooklynmuseum.org/community/blogosphere/2015/05/14/agile-by-design (accessed February 19, 2019).

3. Jake Knapp, John Zeratsky, Braden Kowitz, and Dan Bittner. *Sprint: How to Solve Big Problems and Test New Ideas in Just Five Days* (New York; Prince Frederick, MD: Simon & Schuster Audio, 2016); *also* Kate Haley Goldman and David McKenzie, "Adding Historical Voices to the Ford's Theatre Site: Prototyping Sprint 1, Round 2," *Ford's Theatre Blog* (blog), January 29, 2018, https://www.fords.org/blog/post/adding-historical-voices-to-the-ford-s-theatre-site-prototyping-sprint-1-round-2/ (accessed February 19, 2019); *also* Kate Haley Goldman and David McKenzie, "Following a Historical Figure, Again: Prototyping Sprint 3," *Ford's Theatre Blog* (blog), September 12, 2018, https://www.fords.org/blog/post/following-a-historical-figure-again-prototyping-sprint-3/ (accessed February 19, 2019); *also* Kate Haley Goldman and David McKenzie, "How Relevant Is Too Relevant? Connecting Past & Present at the Ford's Museum: Prototyping Spring 2 - Round 1 (Part 1)," *Ford's Theatre Blog* (blog), April 13, 2018, https://www.fords.org/blog/post/how-relevant-is-too-relevant-connecting-past-present-at-the-ford-s-museum-prototyping-sprint-2-round-1-part-1/ (accessed February 19, 2019); *also* Kate Haley Goldman and David McKenzie, "Learning What Visitors Want: A Shifted Plan and Prototyping in the Museum," *Ford's Theatre Blog* (blog), November 28, 2017, https://www.fords.org/blog/post/learning-what-visitors-want-a-shifted-plan-and-prototyping-in-the-museum/ (accessed February 19, 2019); *and* Kate Haley Goldman and David McKenzie, "Prototyping Historical Figure Cards at Ford's Theatre: Sprint 2, Round 2," *Ford's Theatre Blog* (blog), April 20, 2018, https://www.fords.org/blog/post/prototyping-historical-figure-cards-at-ford-s-theatre-sprint-2-round-2/ (accessed February 19, 2019).

4. Jessica Bathurst and Tobie S. Stein, *Performing Arts Management: A Handbook of Professional Practices* (New York City: Allworth Press, 2010).

5. Colleen Dilenschneider, "Cultural Organizations Are Still Not Reaching New Audiences (DATA)," *Know Your Own Bone*, November 9, 2017, https://www.colleendilen.com/2017/11/08/cultural-

organizations-still-not-reaching-new-audiences-data/ (accessed February 19, 2019).

6. James Chung, Susan Wilkening, and Sally Johnstone, *Museums & Society 2034: Trends and Potential Futures* (Washington, DC: Center for the Future of Museums, American Association of Museums, 2008).

7. McKenzie thanks Chris Evans and Margaret Middleton for this insight during a #DrinkingAboutMuseums conversation.

8. Colleen Dilenschneider, "Cultural Organizations Are Still Not Reaching New Audiences (DATA)," *Know Your Own Bone*, November 8, 2017, https://www.colleendilen.com/2017/11/08/cultural-organizations-still-not-reaching-new-audiences-data/ (accessed February 19, 2019).

9. Colleen Dilenschneider, "Which Is More Important for Cultural Organizations: Being Educationalor Being Entertaining? (DATA)," *Know Your Own Bone*, December 18, 2018, https://www.colleendilen.com/2016/03/16/which-is-more-important-for-cultural-organizations-being-educational-or-being-entertaining-data/ (accessed February 19, 2019).

10. Chad Weinard, "'Maintaining' the Future of Museums: A slideshow on innovation and infrastructure," *Medium (blog)*, December 12, 2018, https://medium.com/@caw_/maintaining-the-future-of-museums-d72631f6905b (accessed February 19, 2019).

11. Kasja Hartig, "Finding a Neutral Starting Point for Producing Museum Experiences," *Medium* (blog), January 27, 2019, https://medium.com/@kajsahartig/finding-a-neutral-starting-point-for-producing-museum-experiences-3ee93c5ada12 (accessed February 19, 2019).

12. Amy Lessen, Ama Rogan, and Michael, J. Blum, "Science Communication Through Art: Objectives,Challenges, and Outcomes," In *Trends in Ecology & Evolution*, Vol. 31, No. 9, (September 2016), pp. 657 - 660.

13. Randi Korn, "New Directions in Evaluation," In Pat Villeneuve, ed., *From Periphery to Center: Art Museum Education in the 21st Century* (Reston, VA: National Art Education Association, 2007).

14. John Cotton Dana, "The Gloom of the Museum," In Gail Anderson, ed., *Reinventing the Museum: Historical and Contemporary Perspectives on the Paradigm Shift,* 2004.

15. Hartig, Kajsa, "Finding a Neutral Starting Point for Producing Museum Experiences," *Medium* (blog), January 27, 2019, https://medium.com/@kajsahartig/finding-a-neutral-starting-point-for-producing-museum-experiences-3ee93c5ada12 (accessed February 19, 2019).

16. Andrea Jones, "7 Reasons Museums Should Share More Experiences, Less Information," *Peak Experience Lab* (blog), March 26, 2017, http://www.peakexperiencelab.com/blog/2017/3/24/7-reasons-why-museums-should-share-more-experiences-less-information (accessed February 19, 2019).

BIBLIOGRAPHY

Bathurst, Jessica, and Tobie S. Stein. *Performing Arts Management: A Handbook of Professional Practices.* New York City: Allworth Press, 2010.

Bernstein, Shelley. "Fighting the Three Dots of User Expectation." *BKM TECH* (blog), May 6, 2015. https://www.brooklynmuseum.org/community/blogosphere/2015/05/06/fighting-the-three-dots-of-user-expectation/ (accessed February 19, 2019).

Bernstein, Shelley. "Learning from Agile Fails." *BKM TECH* (blog), May 5, 2015. https://www.brooklynmuseum.org/community/blogosphere/2015/05/05/learning-from-agile-fails/ (accessed February 19, 2019).

Chung, James, Susan Wilkening, and Sally Johnstone. *Museums & Society 2034: Trends and Potential Futures.* Washington, DC: Center for the Future of Museums, American Association of Museums, 2008.

Dana, John Cotton. "The Gloom of the Museum." In Gail Anderson, ed., *Reinventing the Museum: Historical and Contemporary Perspectives on the Paradigm Shift,* 2004.

Devine, Sara. "Agile by Design." *BKM TECH* (blog), May 14, 2015. https://www.brooklynmuseum.org/community/blogosphere/2015/05/14/agile-by-design (accessed February 19, 2019).

Dilenschneider, Colleen. "Cultural Organizations Are Still Not Reaching New Audiences (DATA)." *Know Your Own Bone.* November 8, 2017, https://www.colleendilen.com/2017/11/08/cultural-organizations-still-not-reaching-new-audiences-data/ (accessed February 19, 2019).

Dilenschneider, Colleen. "Which Is More Important for Cultural Organizations: Being Educational or Being Entertaining? (DATA)." *Know Your Own Bone.* December 18, 2018. https://www.colleendilen.com/2016/03/16/which-is-more-important-for-cultural-organizations-being-educational-or-being-entertaining-data/ (accessed February 19, 2019).

Evjen, Max. "Jazz Hands Out!: Why #Musetech Should Be Like Theatre." Ignite Talk. Museum Computer Network Conference. Denver, CO, 2018. (https://bit.ly/2N0Mb2C)

Haley Goldman, Kate, and David McKenzie. "Adding Historical Voices to the Ford's Theatre Site: Prototyping Sprint 1, Round 2." *Ford's Theatre Blog* (blog), January 29, 2018. https://www.fords.org/blog/post/adding-historical-voices-to-the-ford-s-theatre-site-prototyping-sprint-1-round-2/ (accessed February 19, 2019).

Haley Goldman, Kate, and David McKenzie. "Following a Historical Figure, Again: Prototyping Sprint 3." *Ford's Theatre Blog* (blog), September 12, 2018. https://www.fords.org/blog/post/following-a-historical-figure-again-prototyping-sprint-3/ (accessed February 19, 2019).

Haley Goldman, Kate, and David McKenzie. "How Relevant Is Too Relevant? Connecting Past & Present at the Ford's Museum: Prototyping Spring 2 - Round 1 (Part 1)." *Ford's Theatre Blog* (blog), April 13, 2018. https://www.fords.org/blog/post/how-relevant-is-too-relevant-connecting-past-present-at-the-ford-s-museum-prototyping-sprint-2-round-1-part-1/ (accessed February 19, 2019).

Haley Goldman, Kate, and David McKenzie. "Learning What Visitors Want: A Shifted Plan and Prototyping in the Museum." *Ford's Theatre Blog* (blog), November 28, 2017. https://www.fords.org/blog/post/learning-what-visitors-want-a-shifted-plan-and-prototyping-in-the-museum/ (accessed February 19, 2019).

Haley Goldman, Kate, and David McKenzie. "Prototyping Historical Figure Cards at Ford's Theatre: Sprint 2, Round 2." *Ford's Theatre Blog* (blog), April 20, 2018. https://www.fords.org/blog/post/prototyping-historical-figure-cards-at-ford-s-theatre-sprint-2-round-2/ (accessed February 19, 2019).

Haley Goldman, Kate, and David McKenzie. "Take-Aways While Connecting Past & Present in the Ford's Museum: Prototyping Sprint 2 - Round 1 (Part 2)." *Ford's Theatre Blog* (blog), April 13, 2018. https://www.fords.org/blog/post/take-aways-while-connecting-past-present-in-the-ford-s-museum-prototyping-sprint-2-round-1-part-2/ (accessed February 19, 2019).

Haley Goldman, Kate Goldman and David McKenzie. "Taking It To the Streets: Prototyping Sprint 1, Round 1." *Ford's Theatre Blog* (blog), December 20, 2017. https://www.fords.org/blog/post/taking-it-to-the-streets-prototyping-sprint-1-round-1/ (accessed February 19, 2019).

Hartig, Kajsa. "Finding a Neutral Starting Point for Producing Museum Experiences." *Medium* (blog), January 27, 2019. https://medium.com/@kajsahartig/finding-a-neutral-starting-point-for-producing-museum-experiences-3ee93c5ada12 (accessed February 19, 2019).

Jones, Andrea. "7 Reasons Museums Should Share More Experiences, Less Information." *Peak Experience Lab* (blog), March 26, 2017. http://www.peakexperiencelab.com/blog/2017/3/24/7-reasons-why-museums-should-share-more-experiences-less-information (accessed February 19, 2019).

Knapp, Jake, John Zeratsky, Braden Kowitz, and Dan Bittner. *Sprint: How to Solve Big Problems and Test New Ideas in Just Five Days*. New York; Prince Frederick, MD: Simon & Schuster Audio, 2016.

Korn, Randi, "New Directions in Evaluation." In Pat Villeneuve, ed., *From Periphery to Center: Art Museum Education in the 21st Century*. Reston, VA: National Art Education Association, 2007.

Lesen, Amy, Ama Rogan, and Michael, J. Blum. "Science Communication Through Art: Objectives,Challenges, and Outcomes." In *Trends in Ecology & Evolution*, Vol. 31, No. 9, (September 2016), pp. 657 - 660.

Low, Theodore. "What is a Museum?" In Gail Anderson, ed. *Reinventing the Museum: Historical and Contemporary Perspectives on the Paradigm Shift*, 2006.

Rozik, Eli. "The Roots of Theatre: Rethinking Ritual and Other Theories of Origin." University of Iowa Press, 2002.

Weinard, Chad. "'Maintaining' the Future of Museums: A slideshow on innovation and infrastructure." *Medium (blog)*. December 12, 2018. https://medium.com/@caw_/maintaining-the-future-of-museums-d72631f6905b (accessed February 19, 2019).

Slow Change

Clare Brown
Isabella Bruno

Isabella: On my way to Museums and the Computer Network 2018, I read *Dark Matter and Trojan Horses: A Strategic Design Vocabulary* by Dan Hill. The conference was a reset and reflective experience. As a new Smithsonian employee for almost a year, I was wrestling with its vastness. I talked incessantly to many people at the conference about Hill's ideas on stability and strategy at institutional scale.

Then the government shutdown of 2019 closed Smithsonian museums for four weeks.

Figure 1 Fake t-shirt, designed by Isabella Bruno

Clare Brown and Isabella Bruno: During the furlough we sat down to consider strategic design in museum contexts by discussing the book. Although most museum employees may not be subject to the federal bureaucracies as in the Smithsonian Institution, it is not a far stretch to draw broad connections to the outdated organizational structures, processes, communication methods, and workflow infrastructures that many museums perpetuate despite progress and evolution that has happened outside the museum sector. Dark Matter and Trojan Horses focuses on strategic design within large-scale organizations and projects. Hill explores the notion of "dark matter" as the intangible, invisible systems and cultures which bind organizations together. This dark matter creates sticky problems but it can also be used as a lubricant to help untangle those same sticky problems.

The following chapter, drawn from recorded dialogue, edited for clarity, addresses relevance between Dark Matter and Trojan Horses and the museum context by asking: What is strategic design? Why strategic design for museums? How we can make practical use of strategic design within the museum context?

For both of us, museum process is vital to the outcome of the work we do. Underpinning our daily efforts is an understanding that the modes by which we work affect the products we create. Without explicitly referring to it, Dan Hill builds a thread of arguments that are closely aligned to what is known as "Conway's Law."

Clare: I'm particularly interested in Conway's Law because it's the relationship between how something's made and what the effect of that is on the end product. Conway's law is: "Any organization that designs a system (defined broadly) will produce a design whose structure is a copy of the organization's communication structure."[1] It has been a focus of mine to draw a connection between Conway's Law and museum practice, in order to evolve the methods by which we work together to produce visitor experiences.

Isabella: I'll read a quote from the book. Dan Hill writes "the user is rarely aware of the organizational context that produces a product, service, or artifact, yet the outcome is directly affected by it."[2] Not just communication structure, it could also be expanded to power structures. Toyota subverted the traditional top-down factory hierarchy by introducing the "andon" cord (now wireless button). Workers pull the cord to alert co-workers when a problem crops up so they can get help. If the glitch persists, workers may even stop the line to troubleshoot.The cords are essential to Toyota's concept of built-in quality, or catching problems before they head down the line. There, issues don't have to swim upstream against the flow of communication. In contrast to environments where pointing out what a boss hasn't prioritized inherently undermines organizational hierarchy. Toyota made quality a truly shared responsibility, so mission-critical that it could stop the factory floor.

Clare: Our communication structures, organizational structure, team formation and project management directly affect what we're creating. That is a top-down way of applying Conway's Law. What if we reversed Conway's Law and start with the user experience of the product—or in our case—the visitor's perspective? Visitors assume that everything they experience in the museums is planned and synchronized; what if our organization was structured with an org chart and operating system to mirror the visitor experience? And so why aren't we creating our offerings as a considered whole? I've been thinking a lot about Hill's emphasis on "operating system." An operating system needs to have a relationship to the intended operations as a whole, right? You don't want an operating system that creates something that has no connection to, or bearing on what it is you're trying to do. My view is that many museums have operating systems that are not aligned to the operational goal.

Isabella: In the tech world, I think Conway's Law has been used to encourage smaller teams to work iteratively, agilely and somewhat independently, but there's been pushback over time. Small teams often end up having allegiance to their members over organizational goals. So I've noticed more talk about platforms and microservices as a way to distribute the codebase and encourage more autonomy. Even the term operating system implies that there's some master creator somewhere that created it. And God knows that that's why there's dark matter. Because we haven't yet considered the creation of this system that we operate within. Which leads us to: what is strategic design? How might museums use it?

Clare: Strategic design is a way to approach wicked problems which are tangled networked problems. Dark matter would be the stuff between all those tangles. Museums, whether they are government museums or not, local, experimental museums, art galleries, or public art museums; all have this weird, non corporate, but also "non" nonprofit way of working and complex, networked, organizational and operational problems. We have problems with how to manage collections, storage space, staffing, we are short on money, we pay our people poorly. We have major disconnects between the goals and values of disciplines across museum functions. All of this results in major morale issues—something I hear repeated among museum colleagues both across the USA and in the UK and Canada. We hear this in conferences, too, where numerous sessions are devoted to discussing problems in process and museum culture. Interestingly though, it is rare to hear these discussions move past day to day issues or siloed issues. This is why strategic design seems so necessary in the museum field.

Isabella: Hill proposes that governments need strategic design because they are "18th century institutions underpinned by philosophies and cultures having a similar vintage, now facing 21st century problems."[3] That's two centuries removed! This applies to public institutions, large bureaucratic governmental entities, and the wicked problems of healthcare and education, these large, broad, sweeping societal structures. As Hill says: "The dark matter of strategic designers is organisational culture, policy environments, market mechanisms, legislation, finance models and other incentives, governance structures, tradition and habits, local culture and national identity, the habitats, situations and events that decisions are produced within."[4] So we know our context applies, but as a skill set, is strategic design just for designers? It's got the word design in it. Who is it for? Who can use it?

Clare: That's a good question. Hill spends a lot of time talking about the role of designers and is somewhat disparaging about external designers (consultancy design) versus internal. He emphasizes the downfall of "design thinking," corporatized and systematized in a way that simplifies design too far. He laments the trend of simplifying design thinking to something like 'ten easy steps that you can learn on YouTube' where anybody can be a designer.

Isabella: External designers don't have to live with the reality of implementing their work. It can become a situation in which someone pops by and leaves half-formed tools that sound great but are actually unusable. Or, the organization rejects some recommendations and implements others which leads to lopsided results.

Clare: Yes! What an unfortunate waste of time and money for organizations that are desperate for workable solutions. In addition to discussing the pitfalls of external designers, Hill also expresses concern about the disadvantaged position many internal designers are in. He talks about the importance of design stewardship—fostering and caring for what is intrinsically good in the practice—something that only in-house designers can do for an organization. But he also explains why it is difficult to be a design steward when the organizational and operational system doesn't include the designer to the best advantage.

Isabella: Designers aren't invited to contribute to planning or strategy. Since that's where operation and hierarchy is established, design is in a position that cannot "exert the strategic value inherent in design."[5] We are embedded, but not empowered to share our observations that emerge from our cross-disciplinary, non-linear work.

Clare: He is saying a strategic design gets into the dark matter. But what about the barriers between designers in this business planning and organization? How can we really get at the dark matter? Except covertly, insidiously, but not directly?

It's interesting that Dan Hill is a strategic designer, employed by and embedded within the Finnish government. His use of the word embedded is how journalists are placed in Afghanistan—where they are placed within the situation in order to observe and report about the situation.

Isabella: Dan Hill's role is unique because he is both a part of the agency and also coming in as an authority at the same time.

Clare: I think it would be worth breaking this language into two: embedded and native. Native designers are the ones who suffer from being part of the original organization because they are pigeon-holed into roles and systems that don't maximize their abilities. Embedded designers are deployed or deputized to an organization to observe, maintain perspective, and suggest improvements in roles and systems.

Even as native designers we do have perspective... in fact, it is the strength of all designers to have perspective. Our perspective comes from the fact that we are not subjects specialists in the topics around which we design. We have to maintain the ability to work across projects, across multiple teams, and we see connections because we don't have our heads buried in singular efforts. The challenge that designers have in museums is that we are brought in as technicians to implement what other people want us to do, not because of our strategic abilities. What happens if the question being asked is not the right question? We're not in a position—like Hill is—to make report on our observations in an effort to make strategic change. The problem is that the word "design" is misunderstood, undervalued and misplaced in the museum.

Isabella: I would say that this is probably something that a lot of roles in the museum feel—the value of their role is misidentified. Every profession has gone through a period where their only selling point is the product they deliver. An evolution is necessary for their processing value to catch up to their output value. And it's not a smooth evolution from "Oh, well, the designer's value is their knowledge of the production process," to "designers have actual ideas," and then "designers will be able to talk to people who weren't in the room about the ideas." The definition of value and ability to recognize it expands over time. Once, graphic designer just meant typesetter, not person who deeply understands visual communication. I hope that evolution happens for all roles in museums. Look at what's just happened with the recent conservation efforts for the NMAH pair of Ruby Slippers from the Wizard of Oz. Our conservators were not just technicians, but their forensic vantage point aided in cracking an FBI case for a stolen, then recovered, pair.[6] That's more than a wonderful human interest story, it helps me understand more about what conservation is and can do.

Clare: In order to affect strategic change through strategic design, and the way he described it, it would not be isolated to your own department. It would have to be people who are able to see across divisions. Exhibition designers are uniquely positioned in the same way that collections managers are, because we're not project specific. We are also completely connected to the audience. We move inside and outside of the museum, and across.

Isabella: Reporting structure can be a barrier when it doesn't recognize the overlaps between project types or teams and reward our ability to move successfully between different spheres of knowledge. We context shift as we move between projects. It falls upon the shoulders of each member of the project to translate from one domain or sphere of knowledge into his or her own. And conversely, from his or her own into that of another sphere. As a clarifying example, no one would ever expect to pass unclear plans or expectations to a team of fabricators, and yet we don't think twice about passing half-baked information between educators, curators, designers, etc without a similar rigor. We are missing the benefits of distributed work and network redundancy. We could lower our risk by accepting that knowledge cannot be siloed, if our work is not. To paraphrase from Michael Lewis' *The Fifth Risk*, the burden of education doesn't fall only on the Department of Education—it's the county, the parents, the transportation system, the health board, it's everything that makes school possible.[7] Hill has a metaphor about a building in which many systems run simultaneously, relational but not dependent. Some systems can change faster than others, but slowness of changing all systems isn't obstinance, it's stability. It's why microservices are the new hot thing as distributed, independently deployable applications. It's why government carries risk (nuclear waste storage, superfund clean-up, etc.) that the for-profit world cannot or will not take on. Our time frames are so long (in perpetuity!) the biggest risk seems more likely to be not actively listening, responding to situations and people. We struggle with the soft skills.

Clare: While Dan Hill's case studies were interesting and relevant to museums, I would love to have more practical ways for us to improve our position as native designers. Like curling, we need a person with a brush in front of the stone. One of the ideas we had after furlough—when we came back fresh and ready to roll—was a rubric for a soft skills role, as we called it a "project doula." A team member would provide guidance and support for team-mates as they "labor." We thought shifting the role between the team builds empathy and consideration to others' needs.

Isabella: After illustrating team relationships in spoke and hub diagrams, we saw how easy it was to leave out related staff and stakeholders from team formation.

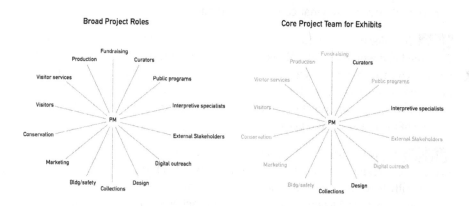

Figure 2 Team member diagram, designed by Isabella Bruno

Clare: And importantly, the visitor consistently was not considered part of the project team.

Isabella: And definitely not Congress! Diagramming who is on a project and noting core and supporting team members exposes our dark matter. Take supporting team members out of the diagram to simplify it and those people disappear. How can we create tools that encourage conscientiousness? In *The Art of Gathering*, Priya Parker talks about by defining the walls of the gathering, but not inviting everyone in; it actually allows us to metaphorically "close the door" and create a safe space for intimacy.[8] Excluding some people is better that inviting everyone. It allows you to bring individuals conscientiously when needed and with purpose, not default to a "committee of everyone." We can create the room and still have a democratic process that allows for movement in and out of the project.

Clare: I like the idea of a project doula reporting out on behalf of you, like a mediation tool. Like a post it note exercise where you ask a question and then you introduce that person to the team: you have to get to know the person in order to speak on their behalf. In *Developmental Evaluation*, Michael Quinn Patton proposes having a new role—developmental evaluator— who reports to the team what's happening within the team and is the emotional barometer of team health.[9] Processes in which we get to know each other and understand individual needs help with the untangling of a wicked problem. Authentic connection unearths dark matter in ways that are not limited to direct questioning but can use intuition and soft skills to find deeper insights.

Isabella: As we talked through this project doula idea, we wondered if we could just listen and document the people we're referring to as opposed to just bring in another wrench to see if it fit the problem. This became a "Personal Journey Map" that asks participants to identify their work steps during exhibition-making, who collaborates or works with them in each step, then their effort level and finally their sentiment. And we are using this to interview 70+ staff, curators, production, conservators, visitor services, public programs, social media, finance, fundraising and more. The result paints this unbelievably rich picture of different roles, experiences with exhibition-making across the museum... and areas for improvement.

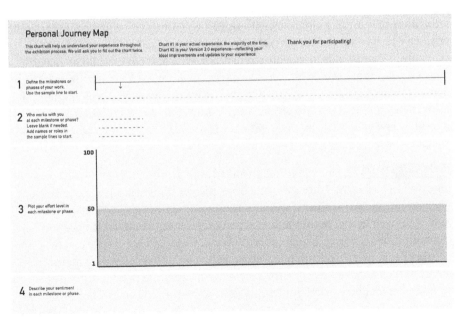

Figure 3 Personal Journey Map, designed by Isabella Bruno

Clare: Because we've gone very broad with who we're asking to do the journey maps, we're extending on both sides the timeline of an exhibition-making process beyond what we assume it to be. For instance, I talked to someone who works on collateral that's related to the exhibitions and her timeline was so very different than anything I experience. I also spoke with procurement staff who I see as integral to the success of an exhibition (we need supplies for fabrication!), but they don't see their daily work as exhibition-related.

Isabella: We realized that we should probably talk to volunteers and docents, who don't technically have any relationship with exhibition making, but they definitely have a relationship with the visitor experience of an exhibition on the floor. So they're doing their own exhibition making in their interactions with those visitors.

Clare: If we think of the exhibition making as what the visitor perceives, front-line staff aren't only representing the museum, they ARE the museum. Our "Personal Journey Map" project is actually a really good 'How to do strategic design' because it is revealing dark matter as we go.

Isabella: And within the limits of our agency. We can't deny that we're milking everything we've got in our current roles by doing these interviews. How we apply strategic design can extend beyond the boundaries of what we think "our work" looks like. We tend to think we're a lot more rational than we really are. But we're not 100% rational, we are emotional, intuitive and many other things. We deserve to bring more of our full, human selves to work. I recently learned of a ritual design practice which has created a funeral to mourn a downsized department for a company.[10] That sounds incredibly strange, powerful and bonding. I'll be really happy the day that I can do interpretive dances in order to communicate exhibition design concepts. I hope we can become open to different modes of communication, using metaphors that tap into diverse experiences that we are each having internally and externally, because just writing memos and grouping post-its isn't enough.

Clare and Isabella: Our conversation ended here but we continue to ask ourselves how we can be strategic designers and bring holistic thinking into our practice and internal culture. We wonder if we can share our design skills outside of our silos (which prevent lateral communication) and across hierarchies (which prevent communication going up when it flows down so well). Can we overtly create networks and lower risk within our organization by strategically working for others' ROI (return on investment)? Would that reciprocate in building trust in strategic design and expand our trust in each other and in our shared mission? We intend to find out.

NOTES

1. Melvin E. Conway, "How Do Committees Invent?," *Datamation*, April 1968.

2. Dan Hill, *Dark Matter and Trojan Horses: A Strategic Design Vocabulary*, (Moscow, Russia: Strelka Press, 2014).

3. Ibid.

4. Ibid.

5. Ibid.

6. Griffin, Julia, "How the Smithsonian Helped the FBI in the Case of Stolen Ruby Slippers," PBS. October 19, 2018, https://www.pbs.org/newshour/science/how-the-smithsonian-helped-the-fbi-in-the-case-of-stolen-ruby-slippers, (accessed January 4, 2019).

7. Michael Lewis, *The Fifth Risk*, (New York, NY: W. W. Norton & Company, 2018).

8. Priya Parker, The Art of Gathering, (New York City, NY: Riverhead Books, 2018).

9. Michael Quinn Patton, Developmental Evaluation, (New York City, NY: Guilford Press, 2010).

10. Kursat Ozenc and Margaret Hagan, Ritual Design Lab, https://www.ritualdesignlab.org (accessed January 10, 2019).

BIBLIOGRAPHY

Conway, Melvin E. "How Do Committees Invent?," *Datamation*, April 1968.

Hill, Dan. *Dark Matter and Trojan Horses: A Strategic Design Vocabulary*. Moscow, Russia: Strelka Press, 2014.

Lewis, Michael. *The Fifth Risk*. New York, NY: W. W. Norton & Company, 2018.

Ozenc, Kursat, and Margaret Hagan. *Ritual Design Lab*. https://www.ritualdesignlab.org (accessed January 10, 2019).

Parker, Priya. *The Art of Gathering*. New York, NY: Riverhead Books, 2018.

Patton, Michael Quinn. *Developmental Evaluation*. New York City, NY: Guilford Press, 2010.

Chapter 12

"Virtual Accessibility": Interpreting a Virtual Reality Art History Experience for Blind and Partially Sighted Users

Amy Hetherington
Peter Pavement

Virtual Reality (VR) has come back into fashion in the museum world – the latest wave of technology has produced a variety of creative responses from the cultural heritage sector and its suppliers. Institutions have employed the technology as a new interpretation medium, aiming to deliver explanations and narratives in an immersive environment. Others have used VR to go "beyond the walls" of their buildings, with a plethora of remote museum tours or digitally reproduced historic buildings made available for virtual visits.

Our company, the museum-specialist digital media development agency Surface Impression, was commissioned by the Royal Collection Trust in London, UK to create a virtual reconstruction of the private art galleries of the Stuart-era King Charles I (1600–1649) alongside an online catalog of the fine art collection that

Charles had amassed. The aim of the virtual reconstruction was to use 3D visualization to attempt to recreate the hanging of some of the most spectacular pieces from his collection, that were housed in a suite of rooms at Whitehall Palace in London. The virtual environment was to be based on historical evidence and documents, that will be detailed below.

Although excited by the subject matter and the use of the technology, we were mindful of the accessibility barriers posed by VR. Surface Impression has been active proponents of digital accessibility for culture and heritage, and we have accumulated a reputation for expertise in the field—especially through our work with disability charities and disability arts practitioners. Virtual Reality poses an interesting challenge for accessibility; on the one hand it is a way to bring experiences to people who might not be able to physically visit a location, but on the other hand, it is a medium that presents barriers to those with mobility impairments and especially to those who are blind or visually impaired.

Project Background

King Charles was an enthusiastic collector of Renaissance art and purchased a large number of works. The art that Charles owned was distributed among his many royal palaces, but he took the (at the time) unusual step of creating a series of dedicated spaces at the Palace of Whitehall in London—"privy" (private) galleries arranged purely for the enjoyment of art. However, these artworks were later auctioned off after Charles' death, and the Palace burnt down in 1698.

The two essential historical documents that provide evidence about the collection, are both inventories of works. The Van der Doort Inventory was a catalog produced by Abraham Van der Doort, a Dutchman commissioned to look after the King's collection. The second, known as the Sale Inventory, was essentially a fire sale catalog, drawn up after the King's execution in order to facilitate the liquidation of assets. The content of these inventories provide details on the titles, artists, measurements, locations, and contents of the art and have been a crucial historical source for art historians for many decades. Royal Collection Trust curator, Niko Munz, had been working through the inventories for years, compiling them into spreadsheets that could be used for data sources and locating art pieces that survive to this day. Combining this data with archaeological studies of the Palace of Whitehall and evidence from contemporary Tudor and Stuart period great houses, we were able to create a virtual reconstruction of three key Privy rooms.

The inventories informed the order and sometimes the position of paintings relative to doors and windows, and archaeology provided dimensions of the rooms. However, many decisions came down to the interpretation of the project's creative practitioners—the hanging height of a painting or the position of a chimney breast relative to the roof's ridge were subjective decisions. The works, however, are mostly still in existence and could be relied upon for accurate dimensions, content and sometimes even framing.

Research & Development

We decided to undertake a small piece of research and development work alongside this VR project for the Royal Collection Trust and investigate how this project could be made more accessible to people with visual impairments.

To assist with the R&D aspect of the project, we engaged VocalEyes, a London-based charity that provides audio description for people who are blind or partially-sighted. Their main work is providing live audio description at theatrical performances throughout the UK, but in recent years they have branched out into museum tours and providing pre-recorded material for handheld visitor guides and apps.

Taking one of the virtual rooms, and working with the Royal Collection Trust curator, a VocalEyes audio describer interpreted both the spatial arrangement of the Privy gallery and the paintings. In one minute recordings, the description encompasses both visual aspects and interpretation of the paintings in a rich, engaging style. For example, Titian's "St Margaret" is described as follows:

> *Saint Margaret, in a knee-length mint-green dress with a scooped neck over a fine white chemise, runs towards us through a rocky landscape, both arms swinging out to the left. Her fair-skinned left leg stretches forwards. Her unseen right leg is presumably directly behind as she steps over a defeated lizard-like dragon that curls across the bottom of the picture [...]*

Figure 1 Scenes from *Charles I, The Lost Collection*. The third of these shows the painting of St Margaret by Titian (next to window). The Royal Collection Trust

As a delivery mechanism for the 3D environment, we chose SketchFab—an online platform created for the sharing of 3D models. SketchFab has an accomplished range of tools and, most importantly, works on most devices. As part of our experiment, we wanted to use a platform that smaller museums could conceivably utilize for 3D projects. However, applying the audio to the 3D environment of the Privy Gallery was challenging—SketchFab supports audio, but triggering playback for this project was impossible. To deal with this, we made use of SketchFab's API (Application Programming Interface) to code an alternative method that would trigger audio for each painting, and we also added some high contrast, large buttons to make navigation through the room easier.

Figure 2 Screencap from the VR showing the large navigation buttons that were added using SketchFab's API. The Royal Collection Trust

To iterate development of our product, we tested the reconstruction with partially sighted participants from a local charity for people who are blind or visually impaired. Our testers were very engaged–trying out the Google Cardboard headset enthusiastically and quickly feeding back positives and areas that needed improvement. Through their help, we were able to rapidly improve navigation, and also that impaired sight does not mean impaired engagement – our testers were not art aficionados by any means, but they all were very interested in the experience and wanted to go further than what was on offer.

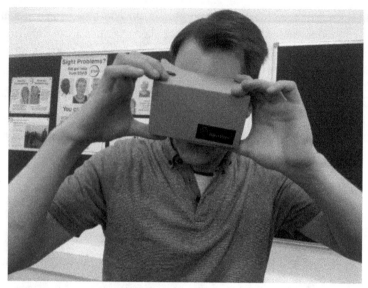

Figure 3 One of our testers from Blatchington Court Trust trying out the Google Cardboard headset. Surface Impression

Based on this project's experience, we are now able to refine both the content and the technical implementation of audio description in VR environments, and we're keen to undertake work to improve other aspects of accessibility in the medium (for example, for those who have mobility impairments). Above all, the experience has taught us that blind and partially sighted users of Virtual Reality are, given the opportunity, as enthusiastic an audience as any other.

Each time a new media technology arises, or, as with VR, is revived, it is often enthusiastically adopted by people working in the cultural heritage sector. However, unlike more mature applications of technology, accessibility practice may not yet be established for the new medium. This poses both a challenge and an opportunity for museums and those who work with them. The accessibility challenges of a new media technology can seem insurmountable, but by working creatively with those that have built up expertise in other fields (in this case VocalEyes) and, above all, with the communities who will benefit from greater access, then opportunities for new techniques, methods, and means of museum communication will emerge.

Chapter 13

AI, Visitor Experience, and Museum Operations: A Closer Look at the Possible

Ariana French

Elena Villaespesa

Artificial Intelligence (AI) technologies bring notable opportunities for museums to learn more about their visitors, play with their collection data and, all combined, influence how people experience a museum. AI and the potential impact of these technologies in enhancing the user experience has had an increasingly important presence in the last few Museum Computer Network conferences. This essay will reflect on the emergence of AI in museums and its role in museum operations as these tools are becoming more widely used. As a result of these reflections, this essay will consider the practical implications of AI and how museums can become informed consumers of these emerging technologies.

The term AI was coined by John McCarthy in 1956 who affirmed that: 'every aspect of learning or any other feature of intelligence can in principle be so precisely described that a machine can be made to simulate it'.[1] This concept has shifted over the last few decades and there have been fluctuations in the application of AI technologies. Nowadays, there is no widely accepted definition of exactly what AI is, and what disciplines are included in the field.

There are multiple classifications of AI technologies[2] and among the most common methods we find are computer vision, machine learning, robotics, and natural language processing. All of these methods offer a way to speed processes which would otherwise involve human labor and costs, such as language translation or image identification. Although we may be in another hype phase of the term "AI," popularity of the tools are normalizing its usage in research and practice. Moreover, while some outputs generated by AI are still very raw and experimental, some applications are becoming an expected functionality by users, such as recommendations, browsing by tags, image recognition from taking a photo or getting a response from a voice assistant.

Museums and AI: The landscape today

Every day, more of our museum visitors' lives are subtly shaped by AI-driven technologies. Within museum operations, AI has the potential to positively influence how quickly and effectively museums respond to these evolving visitor needs and expectations. Two of the main motivations that drive users to a museum's website are planning a future visit and accessing the collection to research, learn, or feel inspired.[3] We can apply these main website use cases to the types of questions people ask to voice assistants, chatbots, or robots, and how visitors interact with museums, using other interactive interfaces. The usage of voice and image search is rapidly increasing. Are museums ready to respond to these changing information search behaviors?

Voice processing and visual recognition are among the technologies classified under the AI heading. However, there are other technologies which offer new ways of interacting with museums and museum data. A search of AI initiatives in museums on the internet, case studies presented in past museum conferences, and journal databases surfaces sixty-one examples (Figure 1). The broad language used to describe AI initiatives makes searching for use cases a daunting task and the true number of examples is most likely greater than sixty-one. Nonetheless, a clear trend can be identified: the implementation of these technologies has really taken off in the past three years. Examples include chatbots for visitor engagement, predictive analytics for visitor attendance, sentiment analysis for visitor comments, and many more.

Two main areas of data analysis in the museum sector are collection information management and visitor research and evaluation. AI can contribute to the enhancement of the collection data with techniques to clean it up, discover new information, create relationships among data sets, or generate classifications and tags automatically. In the area of visitor research, museums have visitor data from ticket purchases, membership subscriptions, website analytics, Wi-Fi connections, and many other data sources. Applying AI techniques to explore, examine and draw conclusions based on this data can enrich the museum visitor's experience. Furthermore, museums are required to justify both their private and public funding and also demonstrate the economic and social impact they have on society. AI can potentially be implemented with this aim of demonstrating meaningful insights into the value of the museum experience and its impact on the visitor.

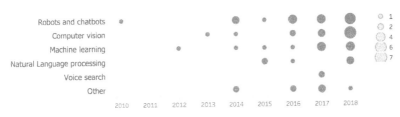

Figure 1 Timeline of AI initiatives in museums (2010 - 2018) (N = 61 examples)

As illustrated in Figure 1, the list of AI technologies is long and, therefore, their potential application in museums is also extensive. We aim to review in this text three key areas where AI is emerging in museums: computer vision for collections information, machine learning for visitor data, and the trending popularity of voice assistants. While the examples listed are far from a full picture of the types of applications for AI, this section aims to illustrate how museums are making use of these tools. Additionally, it aims to provide the necessary context for future reflection about the challenges and limitations of the tools, such as management of these initiatives, ethics, and algorithmic biases.

One of the most promising technologies is the application of computer vision for museum collections. Machines can extract individual elements from the digital object records with a speed that would take humans ages to generate. Running an algorithm on collection data can result in data visualizations of all the object dimensions[4] or the identification of faces or landmarks[5]—offering curatorial staff novel ways of analyzing, researching, and describing museum collections. Insights can be surfaced on new ways of exploring collections by color, for example on the Cooper Hewitt Smithsonian Design Museum[6] and Dallas Art Museum websites,[7] filters by shape and direction of lines, or space and light as seen on the Barnes Foundation website.[8] In another playful example of using AI to generate new ways of collections interaction, the Harvard Art Museum's public API includes machine-generated data in its "Magic Message," where users receive image fragments based on a sentence , or "Face Match" that invites the user to add faces to the corresponding bodies.[9]

While the opportunities for new insights and faster data analysis are tantalizing, AI isn't a "one size fits all" set of technologies. Many applications are still rough and unproven. For example, a complex task for AI is to detect the elements depicted in a museum object to generate subject tags. This possibility has been tested, but results delivered so far haven't been completely satisfactory.[10] Browsing by subject terms brings a valuable way for users to discover objects, but online collections interfaces can be very limited in their ability to integrate these features. While these applications cause excitement in the museum community, there are clear challenges raised from these projects in terms of accuracy and relevancy which need to be carefully considered.

The examples explored so far illustrate how AI can enhance museum collections information. Looking to visitor data as a source for AI-driven insights, we find a growing interest in the sector to use machine learning for visitation pattern prediction and experience evaluation. The volume of user data generated in museums continues to increase rapidly. Data is collected from the visitors' physical experience but also from all the different digital touchpoints of that journey: web, social media, ticketing, and mobile apps, among others. The application of AI to analyze and visualize this data brings an opportunity for museums to better understand their audiences and create personalized and engaging experiences.

For AI to be most effective, there has to be a clearly defined problem to solve. When it comes to museums, traditional data analysis includes audience segmentation, visitation predictions, market research to target prospective members, and visitor experience evaluation. AI brings new possibilities in tackling the examination of these existing datasets, and can also facilitate gathering new data for these purposes. For example, visitor experience has traditionally been evaluated through questioning visitors about their satisfaction. With the aid of AI, analyzing posts from social media or ratings from tourism websites can bring new insights into the visitor experience.

Machine learning, in particular, has been applied to find patterns about visitation in order to predict future trends, to analyze visitors' comments on social media, and identify potential members, among other cases. An example of the usage of external data to discover insights about the visitor experience is the analysis of comments on TripAdvisor. To understand the broad tones of sentiment reflected in tens of thousands of comments, sentiment analysis and topic modeling were applied to generate insights.[11] Sentiment analysis of reviews can be considered a valuable data point in understanding visitor sentiment along with other metrics like an organization's Net Promoter Score, a measure used to gauge satisfaction and loyalty. To bring a more focused understanding of visitor satisfaction, sentiment analysis along with entity analysis can give more detailed insights into how visitors experienced specific aspects of a museum, such as an exhibition.

As in many areas of emerging technologies, pilot projects are essential steps to explore where the opportunities exist for AI and museums. These opportunities are projected to grow exponentially over the next few years.[12] However, as is often the case with new technologies, the hype of the possible can obscure the reality of the feasible. For enterprise-level operations, the reality is intimidating: Many machine learning projects involve significant time and resources to prepare data inputs in a "computer-friendly" format. When considering AI-supported solutions in operational contexts, the value proposition continues to be unclear for many museums due to upfront resource investments and subsequent opportunity costs.

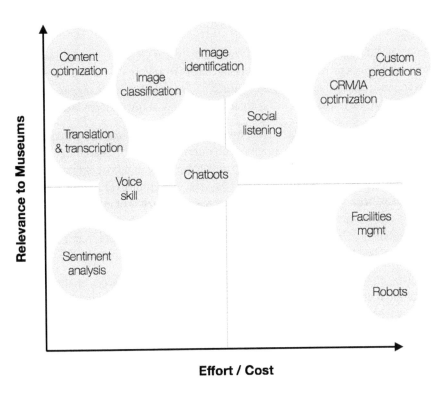

Figure 2 Popular AI subcategories, mapped to axes of museum relevancy and effort/cost.

Figure 2 can be interpreted as an attempt to align relevancy to museum operations against investment for popular AI technologies. It can also be read as a "build vs. buy" comparison, where the left quadrants represent what could be applied with the help of a partner or in-house resource, and right quadrants describing what likely involves a commercial product or partner at additional cost. (That said, any of the technologies shown could be increased in complexity, thereby driving up cost or effort.)

In Figure 2, the areas with high relevance to museums and a lower barrier to entry are *largely related to museum content*. Website text, collection images, tweets, brochures, Instagram posts—and more!—are familiar parts of museum operations. Yet the framing of AI usage in museums is often circumscribed by a "pilot project" approach and isolated from more established digital initiatives.

As barriers to entry continue to drop and use cases become more tangible, opportunities to integrate AI into museum operations may be reconsidered and usher in an era of accelerated change. Today's denormalized and scattered soup of visitor data sources might be tomorrow's engine for AI-driven insights! In the meantime, one change that's well underway is an expansion from touch-centric inputs (like keyboards and touch screens) towards a growing use of AI: voice-assisted technologies.

Apple's Siri, Google's Home, and Amazon's Echo voice assistants (and embedded versions of these technologies in other devices) are among the most popular AI-driven voice assisted technologies. In most of these platforms, query results can be spoken or displayed as text, using algorithms to derive results from web content.

Today, around 20% of search engine queries are voice-assisted, and this number is projected to grow to as much as 50% of all queries in 2020.[13] "Searching the web" and other voice-assisted interactions is now happening in more contexts with the spread of voice technologies in "smart" devices. As AI improves its ability to parse and "speak," the days of touch and sight as primary means of interaction with smart devices and computers may be numbered. Some predict that as AI evolves, more web content will be turned into an on-demand audio experience as it is "spoken" by AI-assisted technologies, creating a new age of content consumption.[14]

Ensuring digital content is accessible to AI-driven technologies is a challenge—an operational one—that's already here. But meeting this challenge doesn't mean starting from scratch; it borrows heavily from best practices in search engine optimization and information architecture design.[15] Unique, authoritative text, video, and images with standard markup (for example, the schema.org framework) is good practice for both visual and voice-assisted search. Along with well-structured content, text that's written in a conversational style supports a more human-like exchange for voice assistant users.[16]

Nearly half of daily voice-assisted searches involve local organizations and the "featured snippet" in Google's search results drives up to 80% of what Google returns.[17] On Amazon's Echo devices and similar assistants, voice query results are limited to the top result, and additional prompts are necessary if more information is needed. The interface for screen-based voice assistants (such as Siri on an iPhone) is likewise truncated with limited voice options to follow up an initial query.

With all of this in mind, visitor information on a museum's website—such as hours, parking information, and accessible entrances—represents a tangible, current optimization opportunity for museums. As the number of AI-assisted platforms, devices, and modalities grow, ensuring that museum visitors receive clear, device-appropriate information in the moment they need it is imperative.

Another imperative is clear, in the dawning age of AI: *There's never been a better time to reevaluate museum-published digital content.* Perhaps more than computer vision, AI-driven analyses of visitor sentiment, and other pilot projects noted here, it's the attention to context and content—how, where, and when museum visitors need information across devices and touchpoints and via different means of consumption (such as voice, keyboard, and screen)—that is a growing and AI-ready opportunity. This is especially true as the museum sector evolves outreach strategies and visitors' expectations are likewise shaped by algorithms in personalized digital experiences.

AI and ethics

Outside the museum sector, machine learning algorithms are being applied in life-changing ways. From judicial sentencing to medical diagnoses, AI can impact human lives profoundly, and not always for the better.[18] AI is a complex set of algorithms created by humans, tested by humans, and trained by humans—and, not surprisingly—retains human biases. Data scientist Cathy O'Neil, author of *Weapons of Math Destruction*, called algorithms "opinions embedded in code."[19] The subjectivity of these algorithms and the inherently complex, "black box" characteristics of AI have led to a precarious reality: AI-generated results that *neither humans nor machines can explain.*[20] As use cases for AI grow, an urgent need for a human-centered approach—including literacy on AI, understanding bias in AI, and all of the ethical implications—grows with it.

As noted earlier in this essay, machine learning algorithms can speed the time it takes to surface insights within collections and museum audiences. The marketing appeal of AI to bring about more nimble operations isn't new to customer relationship management (CRM) software vendors; Blackbaud and Salesforce offer platforms with "AI" components to help museums reach new audiences in record time. But any application of AI in development initiatives should be considered carefully, given known problems of bias and questionable outcomes. Especially where constituent data is concerned, an informed approach to what AI can (and should) provide can help museums ensure that problems are defined sharply, expectations for AI-supported contributions are set appropriately, and resources are invested wisely.

As we face an increasingly technology-enabled future, exactly how AI will change daily museum activities and public life remains to be seen. Museums have long played a role in matters of social justice and occupy a singular position in mediating the cultural dialogue of AI, its impact on societies, and ethics.[21] Continued pilot projects around the applications of AI, dialogue within (and outside) the sector, attention to opportunities in museum operations (such as optimizing content for voice-assisted technologies), and understanding topics like algorithmic bias will help advance this discourse as a fundamentally *human* one.

Conclusion: Artificial intelligence and its place in museums

Any time you talk about an emerging technology, museums have an important role to play teaching the public about it. Artificial intelligence is going to be incredibly important in shaping the world we live in, in profound ways. We need to understand the technology and the issues it raises."

—Elizabeth Merritt, director of the American Alliance of Museums' Center for the Future of Museums.[22]

If the breathless media coverage and accelerating policy talk are any indication, AI will shape lives for years to come. From breakthroughs in medicine to better email spam filters, the applications for AI and machine learning grow every year. In the museum sector, AI offers a range of opportunities, from new modes of engaging with collections to institutional advancement initiatives and beyond. However, barriers to entry can be high before sustainable, operational impact can be proven with many applications of AI; upfront investments to "build from scratch" are out of reach for many museums. In spite of this reality (and in contrast to the hype), there *is* at least one accessible, present-day use case for AI in museum operations: Well-developed digital content is a foundation for engaging new audiences through voice-assisted technologies.

Looking ahead, museums are uniquely positioned to foster dialogues on matters of AI, ethics, impact, and opportunity. If the popularity of AI-related conference topics continues its upward trend and public usage of these technologies likewise grows, we may soon be able to reflect upon the question of museum readiness beyond a "pilot project" approach to AI. Questioning, evaluating, and continuing to push the dialogue on these technologies is a recent but increasingly relevant topic for museum conferences and similar forums, particularly those with a human-centered vision. Without a global authority to regulate the evolution of AI, it's up to an educated public to discern its ethical (and practical) applications. As AI evolves ever-more humanized modes of interaction—through touch, voice, sight, and sound—the museum community can offer an educational and safe space through which to explore the complex world of artificial intelligence.

NOTES

1. John McCarthy et al., "A Proposal for the Dartmouth Summer Research Project on Artificial Intelligence, August 31, 1955," *AI Magazine* 27, no. 4 (December 15, 2006): 12–12, https://doi.org/10.1609/AIMAG.V27I4.1904.

2. "Artificial Intelligence: How Knowledge Is Created, Transference, and Used," Report. Elsevier. 2018, https://iatranshumanisme.com/wp-content/uploads/2018/12/ACAD_RL_RE_AI-Report_WEB.pdf (accessed February 10, 2019); Franceso Corea, "AI Knowledge Map: How To Classify AI Technologies," *Forbes*, August 2018, https://www.forbes.com/sites/cognitiveworld/2018/08/22/ai-knowledge-map-how-to-classify-ai-technologies/#c605fa47773f (accessed February 10, 2019); Peter Stone et al., "Artificial Intelligence and Life in 2030: One Hundred Year Study on Artificial Intelligence," *Stanford University,* September 2016, https://ai100.stanford.edu/2016-report (accessed February 10, 2019).

3. Elena Villaespesa and John Stack, "Finding the Motivation behind a Click: Definition and Implementation of a Website Audience Segmentation," in *MW2015: Museums and the Web 2015*, 2015, https://mw2015.museumsandtheweb.com/paper/finding-the-motivation-behind-a-click-definition-and-implementation-of-a-website-audience-segmentation/ (accessed February 10, 2019); Silvia Filippini Fantoni, Rob Stein, and Gray Bowman, "Exploring the Relationship between Visitor Motivation and Engagement in Online Museum Audiences," in *MW12: Museums and the Web 2012*, 2012, https://www.museumsandtheweb.com/mw2012/papers/exploring_the_relationship_between_visitor_mot (accessed February 10, 2019).

4. James Davenport, "The Dimensions of Art," *If We Assume*, November 2013, https://www.ifweassume.com/2013/11/the-dimensions-of-art.html (accessed February 10, 2019).

5. Sara Robinson, "When Art Meets Big Data: Analyzing 200,000 Items from The Met Collection in BigQuery," *Google Cloud Blog*, August 2017, https://cloud.google.com/blog/products/gcp/when-art-meets-big-data-analyzing-200000-items-from-the-met-collection-in-bigquery (accessed February 10, 2019).

6. Cooper-Hewitt Smithsonian Design Museum, "The Collection," accessed March 1, 2019, https://collection.cooperhewitt.org/ (accessed February 10, 2019).

7. Dallas Museum of Art, "DMA Collection Online," accessed March 1, 2019, https://collections.dma.org/ (accessed February 10, 2019).

8. Barnes Foundation, "Barnes Collection Online," accessed March 1, 2019, https://collection.barnesfoundation.org/ (accessed February 10, 2019).

9. Harvard Art Museums, "IIIF Explorer," accessed March 1, 2019, http://iiif-explorer.herokuapp.com/ (accessed February 10, 2019).

10. Adrian Hindle, "Automated Image Analysis with IIIF. Using Artificial Intelligence for Bulk Image Analysis," *Cogapp Medium*, June 2017, https://blog.cogapp.com/automated-image-analysis-with-iiif-6594ff5b2b32 (accessed February 10, 2019); Shelley Bernstein, "Using Computer Vision to Tag the Collection," *Barnes Foundation Medium*, October 2017, https://medium.com/barnes-foundation/using-computer-vision-to-tag-the-collection-f467c4541034 (accessed February 10, 2019).

11. Ariana French, "On Artificial Intelligence, Museums, and Feelings," 2018, https://medium.com/@CuriousThirst/on-artificial-intelligence-museums-and-feelings-598b7ba8beb6 (accessed February 10, 2019); Victoria D. Alexander, Grant Blank, and Scott A. Hale, "TripAdvisor Reviews of London Museums: A New Approach to Understanding Visitors," *Museum International* 70, no. 1–2 (January 11, 2018): 154–65, https://doi.org/10.1111/muse.12200 (accessed February 10, 2019).

12. Bennat Berger, "AI-Enabled Technologies Could Help Museums Survive the Digital Age," *VentureBeat*, November 2017, https://venturebeat.com/2017/11/06/ai-enabled-technologies-could-help-museums-survive-the-digital-age/ (accessed February 10, 2019).

13. Jayson DeMers, "Why You Need To Prepare For A Voice Search Revolution," *Forbes*, January 2018, https://www.forbes.com/sites/jaysondemers/2018/01/09/why-you-need-to-prepare-for-a-voice-search-revolution/#3322221134af (accessed February 10, 2019).

14. Rebecca Sentance, "The Future of Voice Search: 2020 and Beyond," *Econsultancy*, July 2018, https://econsultancy.com/the-future-of-voice-search-2020-and-beyond/ (accessed February 10, 2019).

15. Therese Sullivan, "Appreciating How Metadata Makes AI Possible," *Building Context*, January 2017, https://buildingcontext.me/2017/01/12/appreciating-how-metadata-makes-ai-possible/ (accessed February 10, 2019).

16. Roger Montti, "Google Answers How to Optimize Content for Voice Search," *Search Engine Journal*, January 2018, https://www.searchenginejournal.com/voice-search-optimization/231319/ (accessed February 10, 2019).

17. Christi Olson, "Voice Search Isn't the next Big Disrupter, Conversational AI Is," *MarTech Today*, October 2018, https://martechtoday.com/voice-search-isnt-the-next-big-disrupter-conversational-ai-is-226537 (accessed February 10, 2019); Saima Salim, "Voice-Assisted Search: The Future of Internet Queries (Infographic)," *Digital Information World*, October 2018, https://www.digitalinformationworld.com/2018/10/infographic-the-state-of-mobile-voice-search.html (accessed February 10, 2019).

18. Jason Tashea, "Courts Are Using AI to Sentence Criminals. That Must Stop Now," *WIRED*, April 2017, https://www.wired.com/2017/04/courts-using-ai-sentence-criminals-must-stop-now/ (accessed February 10, 2019); Jeremy Hsu, "Can a Crowdsourced AI Medical Diagnosis App Outperform Your Doctor?," *Scientific American*, August 2017, https://www.scientificamerican.com/article/can-a-crowdsourced-ai-medical-diagnosis-app-outperform-your-doctor/ (accessed February 10, 2019); Julia Angwin et al., "Machine Bias," *ProPublica*, May 2016, https://www.propublica.org/article/machine-bias-risk-assessments-in-criminal-sentencing (accessed February 10, 2019).

19. Yves Smith, "Data Scientist Cathy O'Neil: 'Algorithms Are Opinions Embedded in Code'," *Naked Capitalism*, August 2017, https://www.nakedcapitalism.com/2017/08/data-scientist-cathy-oneil-algorithms-opinions-embedded-code.html (accessed February 10, 2019).

20. Cliff Kuang, "Can A.I. Be Taught to Explain Itself?," *The New York Times*, November 2017, https://www.nytimes.com/2017/11/21/magazine/can-ai-be-taught-to-explain-itself.html (accessed February 10, 2019).

21. Kate McLeod, "The Role Museums Play in Social Activism," Americans for the Arts, 2017, https://www.americansforthearts.org/2017/08/02/the-role-museums-play-in-social-activism (accessed February 10, 2019).

22. Jane L. Levere, "Artificial Intelligence, Like a Robot, Enhances Museum Experiences," *The New York Times*, October 2018, https://www.nytimes.com/2018/10/25/arts/artificial-intelligence-museums.html (accessed February 10, 2019).

BIBLIOGRAPHY

Alexander, Victoria D., Grant Blank, and Scott A. Hale. "TripAdvisor Reviews of London Museums: A New Approach to Understanding Visitors." *Museum International* 70, no. 1–2 (January 11, 2018): 154–65. https://doi.org/10.1111/muse.12200.

Angwin, Julia, Jeff Larson, Surya Mattu, and Lauren Kirchner. "Machine Bias." *ProPublica*, May 2016. https://www.propublica.org/article/machine-bias-risk-assessments-in-criminal-sentencing (accessed February 10, 2019).

"Artificial Intelligence: How Knowledge Is Created, Transference, and Used," Report. Elsevier. 2018. https://iatranshumanisme.com/wp-content/uploads/2018/12/ACAD_RL_RE_AI-Report_WEB.pdf (accessed February 10, 2019).

Barnes Foundation. "Barnes Collection Online." Accessed March 1, 2019. https://collection.barnesfoundation.org/ (accessed February 10, 2019).

Berger, Bennat. "AI-Enabled Technologies Could Help Museums Survive the Digital Age." *VentureBeat*, November 2017. https://venturebeat.com/2017/11/06/ai-enabled-technologies-could-help-museums-survive-the-digital-age/ (accessed February 10, 2019).

Bernstein, Shelley. "Using Computer Vision to Tag the Collection." *Barnes Foundation Medium*, October 2017. https://medium.com/barnes-foundation/using-computer-vision-to-tag-the-collection-f467c4541034 (accessed February 10, 2019).

Cooper-Hewitt Smithsonian Design Museum. "The Collection | Collection of Cooper Hewitt, Smithsonian Design Museum." https://collection.cooperhewitt.org/ (accessed February 10, 2019).

Corea, Franceso. "AI Knowledge Map: How To Classify AI Technologies." *Forbes*, August 2018. https://www.forbes.com/sites/cognitiveworld/2018/08/22/ai-knowledge-map-how-to-classify-ai-technologies/#c605fa47773f (accessed February 10, 2019).

Dallas Museum of Art. "DMA Collection Online." https://collections.dma.org/ (accessed February 10, 2019).

Davenport, James. "The Dimensions of Art." *If We Assume*, November 2013. https://www.ifweassume.com/2013/11/the-dimensions-of-art.html (accessed February 10, 2019).

DeMers, Jayson. "Why You Need To Prepare For A Voice Search Revolution." *Forbes*, January 2018. https://www.forbes.com/sites/jaysondemers/2018/01/09/why-you-need-to-prepare-for-a-voice-search-revolution/#3322221134af (accessed February 10, 2019).

Filippini Fantoni, Silvia, Rob Stein, and Gray Bowman. "Exploring the Relationship between Visitor Motivation and Engagement in Online Museum Audiences." In *MW12: Museums and the Web 2012*, 2012. https://www.museumsandtheweb.com/mw2012/papers/exploring_the_relationship_between_visitor_mot (accessed February 10, 2019).

French, Ariana. "On Artificial Intelligence, Museums, and Feelings," 2018. https://medium.com/@CuriousThirst/on-artificial-intelligence-museums-and-feelings-598b7ba8beb6 (accessed February 10, 2019).

———. "On Artificial Intelligence, Museums, and Spaghetti," 2018. https://medium.com/@CuriousThirst/on-artificial-intelligence-museums-and-spaghetti-b107cf1b4dc9 (accessed February 10, 2019).

Harvard Art Museums. "IIIF Explorer | Harvard Art Museums." http://iiif-explorer.herokuapp.com/ (accessed February 10, 2019).

Hindle, Adrian. "Automated Image Analysis with IIIF. Using Artificial Intelligence for Bulk Image Analysis." *Cogapp Medium* , June 2017. https://blog.cogapp.com/automated-image-analysis-with-iiif-6594ff5b2b32 (accessed February 10, 2019).

Hsu, Jeremy. "Can a Crowdsourced AI Medical Diagnosis App Outperform Your Doctor?" *Scientific American*, August 2017. https://www.scientificamerican.com/article/can-a-crowdsourced-ai-medical-diagnosis-app-outperform-your-doctor/ (accessed February 10, 2019).

Kuang, Cliff. "Can A.I. Be Taught to Explain Itself?" *The New York Times*, November 2017. https://www.nytimes.com/2017/11/21/magazine/can-ai-be-taught-to-explain-itself.html (accessed February 10, 2019).

Levere, Jane L. "Artificial Intelligence, Like a Robot, Enhances Museum Experiences." *The New York Times*, October 2018. https://www.nytimes.com/2018/10/25/arts/artificial-intelligence-museums.html (accessed February 10, 2019).

McCarthy, John, Marvin L. Minsky, and Claude E. Shannon. "A Proposal for the Dartmouth Summer Research Project on Artificial Intelligence - August 31, 1955." *AI MAGAZINE*, December 15, 2006. https://doi.org/10.1609/AIMAG.V27I4.1904 (accessed February 10, 2019).

McLeod, Kate. "The Role Museums Play in Social Activism." *Americans for the Arts*, 2017. https://www.americansforthearts.org/2017/08/02/the-role-museums-play-in-social-activism (accessed February 10, 2019).

Montti, Roger. "Google Answers How to Optimize Content for Voice Search." *Search Engine Journal*, January 2018. https://www.searchenginejournal.com/voice-search-optimization/231319/ (accessed February 10, 2019) (accessed February 10, 2019).

Olson, Christi. "Voice Search Isn't the next Big Disrupter, Conversational AI Is." *MarTech Today*, October 2018. https://martechtoday.com/voice-search-isnt-the-next-big-disrupter-conversational-ai-is-226537 (accessed February 10, 2019).

Robinson, Sara. "When Art Meets Big Data: Analyzing 200,000 Items from The Met Collection in BigQuery." *Google Cloud Blog*, August 2017. https://cloud.google.com/blog/products/gcp/when-art-meets-big-data-analyzing-200000-items-from-the-met-collection-in-bigquery (accessed February 10, 2019).

Salim, Saima. "Voice-Assisted Search: The Future of Internet Queries (Infographic)." *Digital Information World*, October 2018. https://www.digitalinformationworld.com/2018/10/infographic-the-state-of-mobile-voice-search.html (accessed February 10, 2019).

Sentance, Rebecca. "The Future of Voice Search: 2020 and Beyond." *Econsultancy*, July 2018. https://econsultancy.com/the-future-of-voice-search-2020-and-beyond/ (accessed February 10, 2019).

Smith, Yves. "Data Scientist Cathy O'Neil: 'Algorithms Are Opinions Embedded in Code';" *Naked Capitalism*, August 2017. https://www.nakedcapitalism.com/2017/08/data-scientist-cathy-oneil-algorithms-opinions-embedded-code.html (accessed February 10, 2019).

Stone, Peter, Rodney Brooks, Erik Brynjolfsson, Ryan Calo, Oren Etzioni, Greg Hager, Julia Hirschberg, et al. "Artificial Intelligence and Life in 2030: One Hundred Year Study on Artificial Intelligence." *Stanford University. Retrieved July* 2 (2016). https://ai100.stanford.edu/2016-report (accessed February 10, 2019).

Sullivan, Therese. "Appreciating How Metadata Makes AI Possible." *Building Context*, January 2017. https://buildingcontext.me/2017/01/12/appreciating-how-metadata-makes-ai-possible/ (accessed February 10, 2019).

Tashea, Jason. "Courts Are Using AI to Sentence Criminals. That Must Stop Now." *WIRED*, April 2017. https://www.wired.com/2017/04/courts-using-ai-sentence-criminals-must-stop-now/ (accessed February 10, 2019).

Villaespesa, Elena, and John Stack. "Finding the Motivation behind a Click: Definition and Implementation of a Website Audience Segmentation." In *MW2015: Museums and the Web 2015, 2015.* https://mw2015.museumsandtheweb.com/paper/finding-the-motivation-behind-a-click-definition-and-implementation-of-a-website-audience-segmentation/ (accessed February 10, 2019).

Chapter 14

Teachers Gonna Teach Teach Teach Teach Teach Teach: Capturing the Now-Visible Meaning Making of Users of Digital Museum Collections

Darren Milligan

Introduction

Humanizing, from a digital learning perspective, encompasses our ability, as institutions, to first discover and then understand (to collect, study, and use this knowledge to change our own practice) the creative and educational re-uses of our collections. This includes the information that is created outside our walls, both physical and digital, including when it falls far afield from the interests or comforts of our curators and museum educators. It means we design and support internal cultures that elevate and value co-creation, and develop technical infrastructures to collect and understand what less than a generation ago might have seemed iconoclastic. The contextual multiplicity that is created through collaboration between expert and non-expert, between institution and citizen, made possible through an emerging re-prioritization like this, has an important role in the future of museums. Perhaps more importantly, is its role in the future of education. Humanizing requires understanding and valuing the humans we, as cultural institutions, serve. This seems like a simple statement, but it is one that is packed with significant historical, cultural, and technological challenges.

Our Information Museums

The term 'information society' was first used in Japan as early as 1964, by Michiko Igarashi, who, using the Japanese term *joho shakai*, or information society, or information-conscious society, introduced a phase that would quickly be adopted to describe a society and then an economy in a post-industrial era.[1] Although many nuanced definitions of the term exist,[2] generally an information society is one in which "the creation, distribution, use, integration and manipulation of information is a significant economic, political, and cultural activity."[3] Within this definition, it is clear to see how museums are not anachronistic, but rather a vital player in a society structured upon the use of information. This vital role is one that since the 1960s Americans have more and more begun to expect from their cultural and scientific institutions. Williams describes the change as, "Once the quiet, undisturbed sanctuary of scholars and researchers, museums were seen now as public trusts with duties and responsibilities to their collections, to their communities, and to future generations."[4] Macdonald and Alsford call the museum an "information utility."[5] This definition relies on what have always been described as the key functions of museums, from preserving, studying, exhibiting, and interpreting objects, all roles that involve information about the objects, not focused solely on the objects themselves. Within this context, they call for museums to see themselves as producers of information, that the "primary resources, or commodity, of the museum business as information, rather than as artifacts."[6] This mental framework allows us to easily see the museum's role in an information-dependent society.

But being aware of or acknowledging those using museum information cannot be merely an academic analysis. We need to respect them, their perspectives, and their hopes. We need to value their knowledge as much as or more than our own. Engagement in social media, that is effective engagement, has taught us that this depth of respect can be practiced within the informational roles we serve, as Spruce and Leaf observe, "While museums often focus on 'teaching' the public, social media provides the opportunity for us as an institution to learn. We can learn about our audiences and we can certainly learn from them."[7]

To translate behaviors that perhaps first emerged within the context of online social engagement to the entire growing digital ecosystem of the internet, that is both the breadth and depth of the digital engagement of the lives of our audiences, *is the work of a generation*. It will require both cultural and technological evolutions to achieve. Our digital audiences will always be larger than our physical ones. Always. So, how do we understand our "users," to learn to love them and the work that they do, and to bring their experiences, the contexts that they understand and create, into the knowledge that we protect and share?

Education at the Vanguard

As museums look to document and understand the impact of digitization and digital access, one of the best place to look is in the education space. Understanding how teachers are accessing, creating, and sharing open educational resources, that is "teaching and learning materials that you may freely use and reuse at no cost, and without needing to ask permission,"[8] can allow us to understand *teachers as makers*, as creators, and highlight how we could encourage, support, and collaborate in these efforts. It will give to us a rich understanding of the potential for digital objects that is most in line with our own, that is to facilitate learning, as Parry and Sawyer articulate,

> From temples of sacred objects, to repositories of colonial trophies, and from monuments of civility, to spaces for self-expression and empowerment, the share, the function and the appeal of the museum through history and across cultures has been fashioned by the preoccupations and expectations of each society that has chosen to construct them.[9]

In the late twentieth century museums began to change in a period now referred to as 'new museology,' in which museums were expected to respond to the needs of their audiences driven by the public's reevaluation of the potential for museums to have impact in their education and lives (both locally and globally).[10] Museums began to experiment with the use of digital tools as soon as these tools became readily accessible, going online in the mid 1990s. Soon after, some institutions too began experimenting with how broadly accessible tools, such as the World Wide Web might impact their traditional practices. The public's new expectation for participation has led to what Silverman has called a "third age of museums."

> One that is defined not only by their important and impressive collections...and not just by their roles as educational institutions, museums have entered an age of social service. One that emphasizes the use of their collections...to foster change in our communities, our neighbors, and our world.[11]

Museum-Supported Participatory Culture

From the creation and selection of new pop stars to the scope and contents of museum and gallery exhibitions; access, discovery, and our participation through digital technologies have profound impacts on the designation of what we find valuable in our lives. Historically the process of valuation of cultural heritage was designated solely to official organizations, the museums and other cultural agencies staffed with experts and given the societal and often governmental authority to make these decisions on our behalf. The Web now provides us with opportunities to access and connect directly with these organizations to voice our opinions, share our experience, and play a participatory role in the creation of new cultural information, to act as co-curators.

The accessibility and discoverability of information in our increasingly digitally-enabled world (in the United States, 89% of adults are current Internet users[12]) is important to consider in the space of cultural heritage, one historically tied so closely to limited access to physical objects and spaces. Technologists at leading museums have begun asking, "If you can't Google something does it exist?."[13] Indeed, if we cannot find and understand what is part of our heritage, how can we participate in its designation, scholarship, and preservation? To respond to this, many museums are now devoting extensive resources to increasing accessibility through creating digital "surrogates." Inherent to providing increased access through digitization, museums are also developing mechanisms to improve the discoverability of their content. In other words, putting images of collections online is only the first step in ensuring that digital heritage content is available to the public when and where they need it. To achieve this, they are developing extensive metadata (the structured information that "describes, explains, or locates"[14] a specific item's content) programs to ensure that search engines can direct their users properly. This data is being connected through standards-based programs, like LODLAM (Linked Open Data in Libraries and Museums) who aim to connect professionals and enthusiasts intent on enhancing the usage of library and museum material through improved discovery.[15] In addition to providing their own metadata, they are developing web-based tools to open their collections to their users to create their own descriptive language (often called folksonomies). These user-generated tags have significant impact on navigation and discoverability, and scale when an institution combines its own metadata with this participatory descriptive language.[16]

Participation at Our Cultural Core

Much of what we experience through the web is already mediated by participatory or crowd-influenced efforts. The content and placement of online advertising are influenced directly by other user's interaction with them.[17] The ways we shop online including what items we locate as we browse are directly affected by what we and others have done before.[18] Sites like Reddit[19] use direct methods of user voting and behavioral analysis to evaluate the relevance of and give value to popular online news and content, a role once reserved for newspaper editors or owners. We now live in what Henry Jenkins calls a "participatory culture." He defines it as one with "strong support for creating and sharing one's creations," having a structure for "informal mentorship whereby what is known by the most experienced is passed along to novices," and "where members believe that their contributions matter." This all coalesces within a space in which the members of the culture have some degree of social connection to each other.[20]

The growing expectations for cultural institutions to play an important role in participatory culture are affecting the way they do their work. Museums in particular face difficult challenges[21] as they transition from institutions designed as what historian Ken Arnold would call "containers" for knowledge or culture and "monuments" that provide "a physical permanence as well as an implied symbol of legitimacy."[22] Simon offers a definition of what a participatory cultural institution might be: "a place where visitors can create, share, and connect with each other around content."[23]

Crowdsourcing, as first defined by Jeff Howe in the 2006 Wired article,[24] generally describes the process of distributed or shared problem solving through online participation. Its first implementations may have been commercial,[25] but the term is now being used in many ways in the heritage sector to facilitate participatory experiences with audiences by museums, libraries, and archives. These projects are better thought of as an expansion of traditional public engagement efforts. As Owens defines, "They are about inviting participation from interested and engaged members of the public [and] continue a long standing tradition of volunteerism and involvement of citizens in the creation and continued development of public goods."[26]

The first entirely crowdsourced exhibition was developed by the Brooklyn Museum in 2008,[27] not simply as a popularity contest, but a carefully-designed research project, one built to test the ideas set forth in James Surowiecki's *The Wisdom of Crowds,* that an adequately diverse crowd can make better decisions that traditional experts.[28] This exhibition, *Click!,* explored the ways that the museum's audience, one now expanded by the Web, could participate both by submitting photographic work and evaluating it, in the process of exhibition development. While the exhibition through the lens of traditional art critique was not considered a success,[29] [30] it provided invaluable research data as a model for future projects. It represents that "there is dynamic tension between what the museum wants to present and what participants, visitors, and reporters want to experience."[31] Museums have continued to explore the potential of crowdsourcing in ways ranging from large projects like this to smaller initiatives, however most have focused on collaboration to support the needs of the institution, for example the growth in popularity with volunteer transcription platforms (the Smithsonian's alone reports more than twelve thousand participants)[32] and not found the opportunity for true user-driven co-creation.

Education-centered Participatory Culture, or *Users As Makers*

In 2005, Dale Dougherty of O'Reilly Media coined the term "Maker," not just to describe what is an age-old practice of tinkering and crafting at home, but rather to signify, as Anderson points out, a radical change in the way that our societies and perhaps economies will function in the future: "our tinkering in workshops and garages and kitchens was a solitary hobby rather than a true economic force. That is changing. The world of do-it-yourself has gone digital, and like everything else that goes digital, it's been transformed."[33] But what is a maker? How is the practice of home or community-based creating different now? In her view, Ridge explains that "making" covers a wide range of activities, from fixing something that is broken, tailoring things, making new things, photography, music making, cooking new dishes, etc. It is defined through a process of transition, from merely consuming content, ideas, or products, to producing them oneself.[34] Makers are DIYers, or do it yourselfers, but they have taken what they do and put it online.[35] This digital expansion facilitates connections that would not have been possible in the past. The DIYers have joined together to create a movement. Anderson clarifies, "what turns them into a movement is the intellectual infrastructure that allows makers to reflect on what it means to be a maker."[36]

Makers in Teaching and Learning

The Maker Movement has become an important pedagogical framework in formal education. The *Open University Report* in 2013 includes maker culture alongside emergent forces with the potential to transform education, like Massively Open Online Courses, alternative credentialing (badging), and learning analytics. Making may have a potentially profound impact of how young people learn. In their words, recent changes in networked technologies "enabled wider dissemination and sharing of ideas for maker learning, underpinned by a powerful pedagogy that emphasizes learning through social making."[37] This "constructionism," a phrase coined by Seymore Pappert is a continuation of Piaget's learning theory of constructivism,[38] a process by which learning occurs at the intersection of one's experiences mediated by prior knowledge as well as the experiences of others.[39]

Constructionism—the N word as opposed to the V word—shares constructivism's view of learning as 'building knowledge structures' through progressive internalization of actions... It then adds the idea that this happens especially felicitously in a context where the learner is consciously engaged in constructing a public entity, whether it's a sand castle on the beach or a theory of the universe.[40]

What can be said for the process of making in a different kind of space: a digital space? One example is from the education world and supports the rapid process of classroom change being driven by the growing demands for personalized learning. This evolution aspires to break schools from what has been an industrial-era structure to one more responsive to active learning customized for each student.[41] Growing from this demand, many online lesson plan builders have been developed to assist teachers in creating flexible digital learning resources. Blendspace is one such tool.[42] On this web-accessible platform, users can search from across digital media repositories and aggregators, such as YouTube and Google Images, and collect, structure, and share digital learning resources.

Museum Digital Maker Spaces

The Smithsonian established the Smithsonian Center for Learning and Digital Access, where I work, in 1976 to serve public education by bringing Smithsonian collections and expertise into the nation's classrooms. To understand the needs of teachers, students, and museum educators, the Center spent more than a decade in active experimentation and research, culminating in the launch of a new online platform—the Smithsonian Learning Lab (Figure 1). The Learning Lab is a toolkit that encourages the discovery of more than 3 million digital museum resources, tools for the creation of interactive learning experience based on these resources, and a platform for the publishing and sharing of these new approaches. Since its launch in 2016, hundreds of thousands of museum and classroom educators have used the Lab's tools to create tens of thousands of new examples—ranging from experiments to models—for using Smithsonian resources for learning.

Figure 1 The homepage of the Smithsonian Learning Lab, found at
https://learninglab.si.edu inviting users to discover, create, share, and learn.

Having an in-house platform for observing the behavior of educational users will have important consequences for the Center's work. For the first time, we can see and ideally understand the wide contexts provided to digitized collections through their purposeful aggregation and layering with instructional strategies.

For example, let us look at one artwork, *Electronic Superhighway: Continental U.S., Alaska, Hawaii,* by Korean American artist Nam June Paik. Paik came to the United States in the 1960s and was influenced by the diversity of American culture and also of the technology that spread American identity to people across the world. In the mid 1990s he made this sculpture out of more than 300 televisions and neon tubes structured into a map. Videos playing on the screens within each state represent symbols or ideas, sometimes stereotypes, of Paik's ideas of this America identity.[43] This work resonates with so many visitors because of the obvious geographic connections, and because if its sheer electricity and scale (it is approximately 15 X 40 feet in size). Young and old flock to it and it turns out that it resonates with students in the classroom. Through the Learning Lab platform, we have begun to see, for example, a middle school mathematics teacher using *Superhighway* in a lesson in which students determine the longevity of the work by calculating the lifespan of cathode ray tubes (Figure 2). In another created by an English language arts teacher, students compare the representations of Americans, as shown in the artwork's videos from each state, to how they are represented in a work on contemporary fiction. And in another, an early learning instructor uses *Superhighway*, along with images of artifacts and other museum artworks, to introduce the concept of electricity to preschoolers.

Figure 2 Smithsonian Learning Lab "collection" titled, *Keeping Ageing Technology Alive,* created by classroom mathematics teacher Amanda Riske. https://learninglab.si.edu/ collections/keeping-ageing-technology-alive/A49K2Rcs2wUzD4Rw#r

These non-canonical ways of using museum collections for learning are not necessarily emergent twenty-first century behavior of teachers. In the early twentieth century, the Philadelphia Commercial Museum loaned extensively to Pennsylvania public schools both teaching materials, such as lecture slides and scripts, but also collection objects. We can assume those teachers were using these materials not exclusively as they were designed, but transforming them to best suit their needs.

> ... the materials in the lending collections are functioning, educationally, to better advantage than do many of the class trips to museums simply because the teacher receives her material when she needs it and when it fits into the work being done.[44]

Early research leading to the development of the Learning Lab indicated just this, that most teachers viewed the educational resources designed and prepared by museums as *starting points* for their teaching.[45] What has changed for teachers is both the ease of access to digital resources coupled with demands to design, modify, and teach using open and customizable digital lessons, and for museums is the access to large quantities of data that document their work with this material. There appears to be a great opportunity for museums to connect their collections and goals with those ready to use and make, and to use this information in new ways.

The tenets that define the scope of a space like Blendspace or the Smithsonian Learning Lab: create, share, and connect, are the same that define the maker movement. Connections to content, knowledge, and the tools both for design and production are what create a makerspace, and the connections to others and the sharing of what has been learned and made creates a movement. How do we, as museums, capture and understand all this new knowledge?

Capturing, Understanding, and Institutionalizing Participation

Institutions more than ever are responding to their communities' need for broad access, highly discoverable content, and opportunities to participate in the curating and creation of culture heritage. However, why are so many still slow to adapt to this evolving model? It is simply an opposition to their loss of authority, or as Simon points out, museums may be slow to change due to the lack of data about the impact of these changes, "lack of good evaluation of participatory projects is probably the greatest contributing factor to their slow acceptance and use in the museum field."[46] Obviously, these transformative changes have affected how the public interacts with culture heritage and assigns it value, but how can this be measured? Is the value associated with the educational resources created by a teacher for her classroom on the Learning Lab, for example, the same as that belonging to a curatorial description about a famous and popular artwork?

To Measure and Record It Is to Value It

Simon Tanner, a museum researcher clarifies the question that museums need to be asking in reference to web-mediated experiences by defining value as "measurable outcomes arising from the existence of a digital resource that demonstrate a change in the life or life opportunities of the community for which the resource is intended."[47] This model[48] provides, perhaps for the first time, a clear methodology for cultural institutions to understand how the growing needs for digital access and participation will continue to impact how we define and assign value to our shared cultural heritage and perhaps provide incentive for our traditional heritage organizations to catch up and develop the approaches to understanding and documenting this work.

In a 2012 report, "New Contexts for Museum Information," Nick Poole, the then CEO of the Collections Trust, offered his thoughts on the future of collections managements systems (CMS), the software that museum use to collect all the information known about museum collection objects. He details nine characteristics, in the areas of integration with other museum services, content, and usability, which organizations and those developing CMS should adopt.[49] In the same year, at the Museum Computer Network conference in Seattle, a group of museum information professionals from the Cooper Hewitt, Smithsonian Design Museum and the National Gallery New Zealand Te Papa Tongarewa discussed major trends that have now become common facets of museum practice and the informational needs that they require. Their suggestions call for several crucial additions to account for the growing importance of the public's role in interacting with collections and contributing to the knowledge around museum collections, in particular,

- the importance of linking collection data;

- the workflow around the acquisition, verification, and incorporation of user-generated/co-generated knowledge; and

- the tracking, cataloging, and analyzing of second-generation content

Simon sees the institution as a 'platform' to connect content with creators, distributors, collaborators, and more.[50] The museum, in this context, becomes a culture system that supports, captures, and shares the work of those interacting with the museum resources digitally. The systems that enable these processes and manage the data surrounding them (such as CMS) need additional functionality to support these new types of digital interactions.

In a 2012 presentation at the Museum Computer Network conference, Adrian Kingston, the Collections Information Manager at the National Museum of New Zealand Te Papa Tongarewa, identified three major trends impacting museums, that also impact the mechanisms that we use to manage the data around collections.[51] These trends are no longer emergent, but rather have become core functionality within the museum. First, Kingston identifies the changing nature of what we collect, that material falling under the category of intangible heritage, or those materials that come to collections in digital format or are born digital within our institutions. Second, he agrees with Simon, on the growing role of user-generated, co-created, or user-submitted content. How do we manage and preserve the content (as well as information about its origin, usage policy, etc.) submitted to us through the various digital channels and platforms where museums now operate? Finally, he wonders at the role of object use, beyond how the museum uses a digital asset on its own website or within exhibitions, but rather data about how our digital surrogates (or born digital material) are being used outside of traditional museum functions. These trends are important and need systems and workflows to manage them and ensure that their place within the institution and the contexts they provide are preserved.

Next Steps

As Adair, Filene, and Koloski point out, the current trends in the valuation of user-generated content, or "bottom up" meaning making with the museum stem from the legacy of the decentralization of elite culture and the widening of access that began in the emergent 'information society' of the 1960s.[52] Now though, it is generally acknowledged, and even codified as "Joy's Law," (named for co-founder of Sun Microsystems, Bill Joy) that generally speaking, even at the most elite institutions, the "smartest people work for someone else."[53] Far removed from the once-perceived universal expertise of museums, cultural institutions now recognize that budgets will never, for the foreseeable future, allow the creation of curatorial staffs large enough to adequately catalog, research, much less understand, the vastly diverse collections that even small museums hold. The role that the public plays in helping museum understand the functions and multiple histories of its collections will continue to be irreplaceable in the operations of museum information systems moving forward.

Through digitization, the public is able also to pursue their own goals, to discover, adapt, create, and share what they have made using museum collections. When the public begins using museum collections in this way, truly becoming *makers*, museums must be able to acknowledge, capture, and understand this behavior. This moves beyond the augmentation of what we know about objects to understanding the contemporary use of them in our society. CMS must evolve to ensure that we do not lose the valuable knowledge contained within the understanding of how objects are used, the second-generation content (specifically use beyond our own spaces within exhibitions or on our websites). The information on how an object is used, as Kingston states,[54] should become part of the history of that object.

There is long list of CMS functional enhancements to make this a reality unfortunately, and while some (such as usability improvements) are already part of most software product lifecycle improvements, others (such as tracking of external usage of collections and collection information) have no technological mechanism to build upon. They represent both a change in the institutional acceptance of the value of this kind of information, but also a technological leap in the ability to capture and understand this data. As software companies and museums begin building or enhancing their CMS, it may be helpful to think of them more as "workflow engines,"[55] integrated deeply with the other systems that manage and move data throughout the museum.

Beginning in 2014, the Digital Library Assessment Interest Group of the Digital Library Foundation created a working group to establish best practices for a wide variety of library assessment, including a working group focused on content reuse. Their initial survey concretely describes the challenges facing institutions (in particular libraries, but the same could be said for museums and others) as historical assessment of impact was based exclusively on access.

> These types of statistics do not provide a nuanced picture of how users consume or transform unique materials... This lack of distinction makes it difficult for institutions to develop user-responsive collections or highlight the value of these materials. This is turn presents significant challenges for developing the appropriate staffing, system infrastructure, and long-term funding models needed to support digital collections.[56]

This group, through funding from the Institute for Museum and Library Services will work to develop these standards beginning in 2019.

To better gauge the status of this idea, that is, capturing the *digital life* of museum objects into what might be thought of as an expansion of the idea of a "curatorial file" (that would have historically contained, in a paper file folder, press clipping, conservation treatments, research notes, etc.),[57] I conducted an informal Twitter poll by asking for examples of how museums are currently capturing "non-institutional contextualization of digitized collection objects."[58] Through the conversation, examples of components of the cultures and systems needed to realize this were identified, including interesting work at the Museum of New Zealand Te Papa Tongarewa, Imperial War Museums, Wellcome Library, Horniman Museum and Gardens, Princeton University Art Museum, and others.

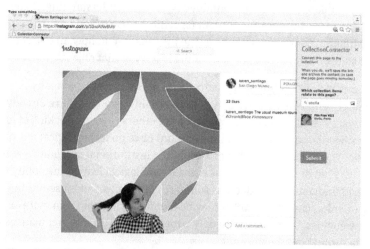

Figure 3 The "Social Collection Connector" concept from the Balboa Park Online Collaborative showing how an easy-to-use browser plugin, coupled with integrated archiving tools and connections to the museum CMS could enable social media managers to quickly collect social behavior and other user-generated content. Design by Chad Weinard, used with permission. https://libp.bpoc.org/prototypes/social-collection-connector

The Balboa Park Online Collaborative has even done some speculative work designing what they called a "Social Collection Connector," a browser plugin that would enable social media managers to connect and capture media observed on social channels (visitor photographs, for example) to the object record in their CMS (Figure 3). The project, like many of those surfaced through the conversation didn't proceed due to lack of funding, uncertainties about copyright and privacy, and, I am sure, an inability for our institutions to quickly, as Chan put it, "embrace the notion of both distributed collections and distributed meaning making."[59]

What we do now know, however, is that this meaning is being made, that teachers are contextualizing museum narratives, and that students are using digital museum resources in ways that are now incredibly visible to us. It feels too that we are on the verge of systems designed to capture and structure this information in ways that help our institutions learn from these new perspectives. Who will take the next step?

NOTES

1. Alistair Duff, *Information Society Studies* (London and New York: Routledge, 2000), pp. 3-4.

2. Frank Webster, *Theories of the Information Society,* Third Edition (London and New York: Routledge, 2006), pp. 8–31.

3. http://en.wikipedia.org/wiki/Information_society. It should be noted that Wikipedia is not considered by the author an authoritative source for information about the information society, but perhaps a definition collaboratively developed, such as the one provided here from Wikipedia is suitable given the subject matter.

4. David Williams, "A Brief History of Museum Computerization," in *Museums in a Digital Age,* ed. by Ross Perry (London and New York: Routledge, 2010), pp. 15–21 (p. 16).

5. George MacDonald and Stephen Alsford, "The Museum as Information Utility," in *Museums in a Digital Age,* ed. by Ross Perry (London and New York: Routledge, 2010), p. 72.

6. George MacDonald and Stephen Alsford, "The Museum as Information Utility," in *Museums in a Digital Age,* ed. by Ross Perry (London and New York: Routledge, 2010), p. 74.

7. Lanae Spruce & Kaitlyn Leaf, "Social Media for Social Justice," *Journal of Museum Education*: 42:1, 41-53, 13 February 2017, http://dx.doi.org/10.1080/10598650.2016.1265852.

8. For additional information on open education resources, see the ISKME OER Commons, at https://www.oercommons.org/about.

9. Ross Parry and Andrew Sawyer, "Space and the machine, Adaptive museums, pervasive technology and the new gallery environment," *Reshaping Museum Space, Architecture, Design, Exhibitions,* (Abingdon: Routledge, 2005), p. 39.

10. John H. Falk and Lynn D. Dierking, *Learning from Museums: Visitor Experiences and the Making of*

Meaning, (Walnut Creek: Altamira, 2000), p. 219.

11. Lois H. Silverman, "Social Work of Museums," Online Video, *Bunker Ljubljana,* http://vimeo.com/19213313 (accessed February 10, 2019).

12. Pew Internet and American Life Project (May 2013), http://www.pewinternet.org/fact-sheet/internet-broadband/ (accessed February 10, 2019).

13. Charlotte Sexton, "@sdarrough says "If you can't Google something does it exist?" #mcn2012moma #mcn2012," Twitter, 10 November 2012, https://twitter.com/cb_sexton/status/267327816406794242 (accessed February 10, 2019).

14. National Information Standards Organization, *Understanding Metadata,* (Bethesda: NISO Press, 2004), http://www.niso.org/publications/press/UnderstandingMetadata.pdf (accessed February 10, 2019).

15. John Voss, "About LODAM," http://lodlam.net/about/.

16. Seb Chan, "Tagging and Searching – Serendipity and museum collection databases," in J. Trant and D. Bearman (eds.). *Museums and the Web 2007: Proceedings,* Toronto: Archives & Museum Informatics, 1 March, 2007, http://www.museumsandtheweb.com/mw2007/papers/chan/chan.html (accessed February 10, 2019).

17. For additional information on one mechanism of online advertising, see the frequently asked questions for Google Adwords at http://www.google.com/adwords/how-it-works/faq.html.

18. For additional information on Amazon's recommendation engine see http://tech.fortune.cnn.com/2012/07/30/amazon-5/.

19. For additional information on how Reddit displays content, see http://www.reddit.com/wiki/faq.

20. Henry Jenkins, "Confronting the Challenges of Participatory Culture: Media Education for the 21st Century (Part One)," Confessions of an Aca-Fan, 20 October 2006, http://henryjenkins.org/2006/10/confronting_the_challenges_of.html (accessed February 10, 2019).

21. Susan Cairns, "Mutualizing Museum Knowledge: Folksonomies and the Changing Shape of Expertise," *Curator: The Museum Journal,* 56: 107–119, 7 January 2013, http://onlinelibrary.wiley.com/doi/10.1111/cura.12011/full (accessed February 10, 2019).

22. Ken Arnold, *Cabinets for the Curious: Looking Back at Early English Museums,* (Hants and Burlington: Ashgate Publishing, 2006), p. 5.

23. Nina Simon, *The Participatory Museum,* (Santa Cruz: Museum 2.0, 2010), p. preface, http://www.participatorymuseum.org/preface/ (accessed February 10, 2019).

24. Jeff Howe, "The rise of crowdsourcing," *Wired* 14(06), 14 June 2006, http://www.wired.com/wired/archive/14.06/crowds.html (accessed February 10, 2019).

25. Daren C. Brabham, "Crowdsourcing and Governance," Confessions of an Aca-Fan, 10 August

2009, http://henryjenkins.org/2009/08/get_ready_to_participate_crowd.html (accessed February 10, 2019).

26. Trevor Owens, "The Crowd and the Library," Trevor Owens, 20 May 2012, http://www.trevorowens.org/2012/05/the-crowd-and-the-library/ (accessed February 10, 2019).

27. Elizabeth Merritt, "Crowdsource the Museum?," Center for the Future of Museums Blog, 20 August 2009, http://futureofmuseums.blogspot.com/2009/08/crowsource-museum.html (accessed February 10, 2019).

28. Click! A Crowd-curated Exhibition, Temporary Exhibition, 27 June to 10 August, 2007, Brooklyn Museum, Brooklyn.

29. Ken Johnson, "3,344 People May Not Know Art but Know What They Like," New York Times, 4 July 2008, http://www.nytimes.com/2008/07/04/arts/design/04clic.html (accessed February 10, 2019).

30. Robin Givhan, "Proles vs. Pros: An Experiment In Curating," The Washington Post, 6 July 2008, http://www.washingtonpost.com/wp-dyn/content/article/2008/07/03/AR2008070301509.html (accessed February 10, 2019).

31. Nina Simon, "Why Click! is My Hero (What Museum Innovation Looks Like)," Museum 2.0, 11 July 2008, http://museumtwo.blogspot.com/2008/07/why-click-is-my-hero-what-museum.html (accessed February 10, 2019).

32. For more information on the Smithsonian Transcription Center, see https://transcription.si.edu/.

33. Chris Anderson, "20 Years of Wired: Maker movement," Wired, 2 May 2013, http://www.wired.co.uk/magazine/archive/2013/06/feature-20-years-of-wired/maker-movement.

34. Mia Ridge, "Bringing maker culture to cultural organisations," Online Video, VALA - Libraries, Technology and the Future Inc., 6 February 2014, http://www.vala.org.au/index.php?option=com_content&view=article&id=802&catid=139&Itemid=402 (accessed February 10, 2019).

35. Chris Anderson, Makers, The New Industrial Revolution (New York: Crown Business, 2012), p. 21.

36. Evgeny Morozo, "Making It: Pick up a spot welder and join the revolution," The New Yorker, 13 January 2014, http://www.newyorker.com/magazine/2014/01/13/making-it-2 (accessed February 10, 2019).

37. Mike Sharples, Innovating Pedagogy 2013: Open University Innovation Report 2, (Milton Keynes: The Open University), p. 5.

38. Edith Ackermann, "Piaget's Constructivism, Papert's Constructionism: What's the difference?," Future of Learning, http://learning.media.mit.edu/content/publications/EA.Piaget%20_%20Papert.pdf (accessed February 10, 2019).

39. Martin Ryder, "The Cyborg and the Noble Savage: Ethics in the war on information poverty," *Handbook of Research on Technoethics,* (IGC Global, 2008), http://carbon.ucdenver.edu/~mryder/savage.html#def_constructivism (accessed February 10, 2019).

40. Ackermann, "Piaget's Constructivism, Papert's Constructionism: What's the difference?

41. Craig Deeda, Thomas M. Leskob, and Valerie Lovejoy, "Teacher adaptation to personalized learning spaces," *Teacher Development: An international journal of teachers' professional development,* Volume 18, Issue 3, 7 July 2014.

42. For additional information on Tes Blendspace, see https://www.tes.com/lessons.

43. National Portrait Gallery, National Portrait Gallery/Smithsonian American Art Museum Commemorative Guide (LaJolla, CA: Beckon Books, 2015).

44. K.A. Wolfrom, "The Rise and Fall of the Philadelphia Commercial Museum: How a Forgotten Museum Forever Altered American Industry," *Independence Seaport Museum,* http://www.phillyseaport.org/rise-fall-philadelphia-commercial-museum (accessed February 10, 2019).

45. J. Ito and L. Langa, "Remedial Evaluation of the Materials Distributed at the Smithsonian Institution's Annual Teachers' Night," *Smithsonian Center for Education Museum Studies.*

46. Nina Simon, *The Participatory Museum,* (Santa Cruz: Museum 2.0, 2010), p. Chapter 10, http://www.participatorymuseum.org/chapter10/ (accessed February 10, 2019).

47. Simon Tanner, "The Balanced Value Impact Model," When the data hits the fan!, 23 October 2012, http://simon-tanner.blogspot.com/2012/10/the-balanced-value-impact-model.html (accessed February 10, 2019).

48. See the Balanced Value Impact Model, from the King's Digital Consultancy Service, accessible at http://www.kdcs.kcl.ac.uk/innovation/impact.html.

49. Nick Poole, *New Contexts for Museum Information* (London: Collections Trust, 2012), pp. 5–6.

50. Nina Simon, The Participatory Museum, chapter 1.

51. "MCN 2012: The Future of Collections Management Systems," Online Video, *Museum Computer Network,* 1 May 2013, https://www.youtube.com/watch?v=93cR1vqY3Xk.

52. Bill Adair, Benjamin Filene, and Laura Koloski, "Introduction," *Letting Go? Sharing Historical Authority in a User-Generated World* (Philadelphia: The Pew Center for Arts & Heritage, 2011), p. 11.

53. Lewis DVorkin, "Forbes Contributors Talk About Our Model for Entrepreneurial Journalism," *Forbes,* 1 December 2011, http://www.forbes.com/sites/lewisdvorkin/2011/12/01/forbes-contributors-talk-about-our-model-for-entrepreneurial-journalism/ (accessed February 10, 2019).

54. "MCN 2012: The Future of Collections Management Systems," Online Video, *Museum Computer*

Network, 1 May 2013, https://www.youtube.com/watch?v=93cR1vqY3Xk (accessed February 10, 2019).

55. Nick Poole, *New Contexts for Museum Information*, 5.

56. Digital Library Assessment Interest Group, "Setting a Foundation for Assessing Content Reuse: A White Paper From the Developing a Framework for Measuring Reuse of Digital Objects project," 25 September 2018, https://osf.io/y9ghc/ (accessed February 10, 2019).

57. For an example of how one institution, the Folger Shakespeare Library describes their curatorial files, see https://folgerpedia.folger.edu/Curatorial_files (accessed February 10, 2019).

58. Darren Milligan, "Trying to source some examples, anecdotes, or writing on how museums capture (like in their CIS, etc.) non-institutional contextualization of digitized collection objects. This might include: external publishing platforms, social media activity, educational uses. (Please RT)," Twitter, 9 January 2019, https://twitter.com/DarrenMilligan/status/1083012231720247296 (accessed February 10, 2019).

59. Seb Chan, "Seems like this is a job for @webrecorder_io and integrating that with a CI/M/S. And embracing the notion of both distributed collections and distributed meaning making," Twitter, 9 January 2019, https://twitter.com/sebchan/status/1083174497543348224 (accessed February 10, 2019).

BIBLIOGRAPHY

Ackermann, Edith. "Piaget's Constructivism, Papert's Constructionism: What's the difference?." *Future of Learning*, n.d. http://learning.media.mit.edu/content/publications/EA.Piaget%20_%20Papert.pdf (accessed February 10, 2019).

Adair, Bill, *et. al.* "Introduction." in *Letting Go? Sharing Historical Authority in a User-Generated World*. Philadelphia: The Pew Center for Arts & Heritage, 2011.

Anderson, Chris. *Makers, The New Industrial Revolution*. New York: Crown Business, 2012.

Anderson, Chris. "20 Years of Wired: Maker movement." *Wired*. 2 May 2013. http://www.wired.co.uk/magazine/archive/2013/06/feature-20-years-of-wired/maker-movement (accessed February 10, 2019).

Arnold, Ken. *Cabinets for the Curious: Looking Back at Early English Museum*. Hants and Burlington: Ashgate Publishing, 2006.

Brabham, Daren C. "Crowdsourcing and Governance." *Confessions of an Aca-Fan,* 10 August 2009. http://henryjenkins.org/2009/08/get_ready_to_participate_crowd.html (accessed February 10, 2019).

Cairns, Susan. "Mutualizing Museum Knowledge: Folksonomies and the Changing Shape of Expertise." *Curator: The Museum Journal,* 56 (7 January 2013): 107–119. http://onlinelibrary.wiley.com/doi/10.1111/cura.12011/full.

Chan, Seb. Twitter Post. 9 January 2019, 7:31 p.m., https://twitter.com/sebchan/status/1083174497543348224 (accessed February 10, 2019).

Chan, Seb. "Tagging and Searching – Serendipity and museum collection databases." in *Museums and the Web 2007: Proceedings,* edited by J. Trant and D. Bearman. Toronto: Archives & Museum Informatics, 1 March, 2007. http://www.museumsandtheweb.com/mw2007/papers/chan/chan.html (accessed February 10, 2019).

Click! A Crowd-curated Exhibition. Temporary Exhibition. (27 June to 10 August, 2007) Brooklyn Museum, Brooklyn, New York.

Deeda, Craig, Leskob, Thomas M., and Lovejoy, Valerie. "Teacher adaptation to personalized learning spaces." *Teacher Development: An international journal of teachers' professional development,* Volume 18, Issue 3 (7 July 2014).

Digital Library Assessment Interest Group. *Setting a Foundation for Assessing Content Reuse: A White Paper From the Developing a Framework for Measuring Reuse of Digital Objects project.* Digital Library Federation, 2018. https://osf.io/y9ghc/ (accessed February 10, 2019).

Duff, Alistair. *Information Society Studies.* London and New York: Routledge, 2000.

DVorkin, Lewis. "Forbes Contributors Talk About Our Model for Entrepreneurial Journalism." *Forbes.* 1 December 2011. http://www.forbes.com/sites/lewisdvorkin/2011/12/01/forbes-contributors-talk-about-our-model-for-entrepreneurial-journalism/ (accessed February 10, 2019).

Falk, John H., and Dierking, Lynn D. *Learning from Museums: Visitor Experiences and the Making of Meaning.* Walnut Creek, CA: Altamira, 2000.

Givhan, Robin. "Proles vs. Pros: An Experiment In Curating." *The Washington Post.* 6 July 2008. http://www.washingtonpost.com/wp-dyn/content/article/2008/07/03/AR2008070301509.html (accessed February 10, 2019).

Howe, Jeff. "The rise of crowdsourcing." *Wired* 14(06). June 2006. http://www.wired.com/wired/archive/14.06/crowds.html (accessed February 10, 2019).

Ito, J., and L. Langa. *Remedial Evaluation of the Materials Distributed at the Smithsonian Institution's Annual Teachers' Night.* Washington, D.C.: Smithsonian Center for Education Museum Studies, 2010.

Jenkins, Henry. "Confronting the Challenges of Participatory Culture: Media Education for the 21st Century (Part One)." *Confessions of an Aca-Fan.* 20 October 2006. http://henryjenkins.org/2006/10/confronting_the_challenges_of.html (accessed February 10, 2019).

Johnson, Ken. "3,344 People May Not Know Art but Know What They Like." *New York Times.* 4 July 2008. http://www.nytimes.com/2008/07/04/arts/design/04clic.html (accessed February 10, 2019).

MacDonald, George, and Alsford, Stephen. "The Museum as Information Utility." in *Museums in a Digital Age,* edited. by Ross Perry. London and New York: Routledge, 2010.

"MCN 2012: The Future of Collections Management Systems." YouTube video. Posted by "Museum Computer Network," 1 May 2013, https://www.youtube.com/watch?v=93cR1vqY3Xk (accessed February 10, 2019).

Merritt, Elizabeth. "Crowdsource the Museum?." *Center for the Future of Museums Blog*. 20 August 2009. http://futureofmuseums.blogspot.com/2009/08/crowsource-museum.html (accessed February 10, 2019).

Darren Milligan, Twitter post, 9 January 2019, 8:46 a.m., https://twitter.com/DarrenMilligan/status/1083012231720247296 (accessed February 10, 2019).

Morozo, Evgeny. "Making It: Pick up a spot welder and join the revolution." *The New Yorker*. 13 January 2014. http://www.newyorker.com/magazine/2014/01/13/making-it-2 (accessed February 10, 2019).

National Information Standards Organization. *Understanding Metadata*. Bethesda: NISO Press, 2004. http://www.niso.org/publications/press/UnderstandingMetadata.pdf (accessed February 10, 2019).

National Portrait Gallery. *National Portrait Gallery/Smithsonian American Art Museum Commemorative Guide*. LaJolla, CA: Beckon Books, 2015.

Owens, Trevor. "The Crowd and the Library." *Trevor Owens Blog*. 20 May 2012. http://www.trevorowens.org/2012/05/the-crowd-and-the-library/LaJolla, CA: .

Poole, Nick. *New Contexts for Museum Information*. London: Collections Trust, 2012.

Parry, Ross, and Sawyer, Andrew. "Space and the machine, Adaptive museums, pervasive technology and the new gallery environment." *Reshaping Museum Space, Architecture, Design, Exhibitions*. Abingdon: Routledge, 2005.

Ridge, Mia. "Bringing maker culture to cultural organisations." online video. *VALA - Libraries, Technology and the Future Inc.*, 6 February 2014. http://www.vala.org.au/index.php?option=com_content&view=article&id=802&catid=139&Itemid=402 (accessed February 10, 2019).

Ryder, Martin. "The Cyborg and the Noble Savage: Ethics in the war on information poverty." in *Handbook of Research on Technoethics*. IGC Global, 2008. http://carbon.ucdenver.edu/~mryder/savage.html#def_constructivism (accessed February 10, 2019).

Sexton, Charlotte. Twitter post, 10 November 2012, 12:08 p.m. https://twitter.com/cb_sexton/status/267327816406794242 (accessed February 10, 2019).

Sharples, Mike. *Innovating Pedagogy 2013: Open University Innovation Report 2*. Milton Keynes: The Open University.

Silverman, Lois H. "Social Work of Museums." Online Video. *Bunker Ljubljana*. http://vimeo.com/19213313 (accessed February 10, 2019).

Simon, Nina. *The Participatory Museum*. Santa Cruz: Museum 2.0, 2010.

Simon, Nina. "Why Click! is My Hero (What Museum Innovation Looks Like)." *Museum 2.0.* 11 July 2008. http://museumtwo.blogspot.com/2008/07/why-click-is-my-hero-what-museum.html (accessed February 10, 2019).

Spruce, Lanae, and Kaitlyn Leaf. 'Social Media for Social Justice.' *Journal of Museum Education,* 42:1 (13 February 2017), 41-53. http://dx.doi.org/10.1080/10598650.2016.1265852.

Tanner, Simon. "The Balanced Value Impact Model." *When the data hits the fan!.* 23 October 2012. http://simon-tanner.blogspot.com/2012/10/the-balanced-value-impact-model.html (accessed February 10, 2019).

Webster, Frank. *Theories of the Information Society,* Third Edition. London and New York: Routledge, 2006.

Williams, David. "A Brief History of Museum Computerization." in *Museums in a Digital Age*, edited by Ross Perry. London and New York: Routledge, 2010.

Wolfrom, K. A. "The Rise and Fall of the Philadelphia Commercial Museum: How a Forgotten Museum Forever Altered American Industry." *Independence Seaport Museum*. 2011. http://www.phillyseaport.org/rise-fall-philadelphia-commercial-museum (accessed February 10, 2019).

Chapter 15

When a Summer Camp, Innovation Hub and an Herbarium Meet: How Steam Collaboration Can Build a Humanized Experience with Technology

Castle U. Kim

Introduction

In March 2018, MCN announced the 2018 conference theme was *Humanizing the Digital*, and called for sessions that would inspire discussion around making technology culture more human in museums.[1] One idea grabbed my attention in the theme announcement: "using technology to build empathy, foster dialogue, and inspire positive change."[2] Without a doubt, museums have been integrating digital technology to engage visitors in empathy, dialogue, and change. However, how about the visitors directly interacting with the technology, for example in makerspaces and with maker technologies, at a museum?

There has been a convergence between museums and the maker movement. Museums, like the New York Hall of Science[3] and Newark Museum,[4] have developed their own makerspaces. The Institute of Museum and Library Services have recognized the value of making and launching the *Making & Learning* project.[5] There was even a session titled, "What's the Point of a Museum Maker Space?" at the 2012 MCN conference. Makerspaces emphasizes informal self-dedicated learning opportunities, but what if visitors could be guided to have a more wholesome and human experience through the maker technology?

The following is a reflection on the collaborative project I presented at MCN 2018. The project was a collaboration between a summer camp, Florida State Universities Innovation Hub and Robert K. Godfrey Herbarium that integrated arts, maker tech, museum specimen, and scientific research.

STEAM

The idea of integrating art with STEM, also known as STEAM (Science, Technology, Engineering, Arts, and Mathematics), was brought up in response to the STEM initiative.[6] Championed by John Maeda[7] and the Rhode Island School of Design,[8] STEAM has been researched by many researchers. Generally, research around STEAM focuses on building problem solving, fearlessness, and critical thinking skills.[9] However, there is another core idea of STEAM that is often forgotten: how STEAM fosters creativity.[10]

In a study published by Microsoft, it showed that 85 percent of young woman and girls view themselves as creative individuals, only 34 percent of them thought STEM jobs involved creativity, while 69 percent of them wanted a career that helped the world.[11] Based on this data, a gap between creativity and STEM. STEAM could be the key to bridge the gap between creativity and STEM. However, balancing all the aspect of STEAM is difficult. It is a challenge to create a properly balanced STEAM program, so what if different institutions with different areas of expertise came together to create a STEAM program?

The Innovation Hub at Florida State University

The Innovation Hub (The Hub) at Florida State University is a new facility that opened in March of 2018. The Hub's mission is to "foster a collaborative community founded on a culture of creativity and innovation ... using design thinking and emerging technologies."[12] The fablab at the Hub features twenty plus 3D printers, a laser cutter, vinyl cutter, and other innovation technologies. During the school year, The Hub focuses on being a resource to FSU and during the summer the Innovation Hub expanse its focus to the Tallahassee community, such as creating K-12 educational outreach programs.[13]

More information about the Hub can be found at the Hub's website: https://innovation.fsu.edu/.

The STEAM-ing Collaboration

In the summer of 2018 Innovation Hub, FSU's Robert K. Godfrey Herbarium, and a local summer camp collaborated for a STEAM experience for the students. The goal of the program was to show different ways creativity is involved in STEM.

The day started at the Robert K. Godfrey Herbarium, where over 220,000 museum-quality plant and microalgae specimen collection, and original scientific illustration used in books and publications are housed.[14] The students learned about the relevance of plant pressing in research today, scientific illustrations, and how to press plants. Through the Herbarium the students experienced how art and creativity is part of scientific research, such as how do you position a plant on a page, so it fits and best represent the plant. Following the Herbarium, the campers visited and toured The Hub. Then the students engaged in a nature-inspired activity that involved 3D modeling, 3D printing, and laser cutting. Using TinkerCAD, a free web-based 3D modeling software, the campers modeled nature inspired tokens (which later was 3D printed at the Hub). After 3D modeling, the campers were asked to draw a 'scientific illustration' throughout the week. The campers would select one on their illustrations. The selected illustration was converted digitally with Adobe Illustrator, and then the illustration was laser cut into a wooden costar for the campers to take home.

Conclusion

In 2014, McGrath predicted that people will look to organizations to "create complete and meaningful experiences."[15] This has been becoming the expectations visitors have with museums: to have a wholesome human experience. For museum visitors who are directly interreacting with technology, as more opportunities are arising with the development of museum makerspaces, could have a deeper experience if they are involved in STEAM program. A singular institution is often an expert on something and not all thing, it would have been impossible if the summer camp, The Hub, or the Herbarium tried to build this program on its own. A true STEAM program could provide a wholesome experience where museums and technology feel more human as the visitors are free to be creative. Perhaps one way to humanize the digital, specifically the digital and technology visitors directly interact with, is to engage visitors in empathy, dialogue, and change through collaborative STEAM projects.

NOTES

https://innovation.fsu.edu/.

1. Adrienne Lalli Hills, Rob Weisberg, and Catherine Devine, "MCN2018: Humanizing the Digital," *Museum Computer Network* (blog), March 6, 2018, http://mcn.edu/mcn-2018-humanizing-the-digital/ (accessed February 25, 2019).

2. Ibid.

3. "Maker Space." *New York Hall of Science*, https://nysci.org/make/maker-space/ (accessed February 25, 2019).

4. "MakerSPACE at Newark Museum," *Newark Museum*, https://www.newarkmuseum.org/makerspace (accessed February 25, 2019).

5. "Making," *Institute of Museum and Library Services*, https://www.imls.gov/issues/national-issues/making (accessed February 25, 2019).

6. Lisa Catterall, "A Brief History of STEM and STEAM from an Inadvertent Insider," *The STEAM Journal*, 3, no. 1 (2017). DOI: 10.5642/steam.20170301.05

7. Ibid.

8. "Rhode Island School of Design Launches STEAM Map to Demonstrate Global Activity and Support for the Movement," *Rhode Island School of Design*, https://www.risd.edu/news/for-press/press-releases/rhode-island-school-of-design-launches-steam-map-to-demonstrate-global-activity-and-support-for-the-movement/ (accessed February 10, 2019).

9. John Maeda, "STEM + Art = STEAM." The STEAM Journal 1, no. 1 (2013). DOI: 10.5642/steam.201301.34

10. Nicole Radiziwil, Morgan Benton, and Cassidy Moellers, "From STEM to STEAM: Reframing What it Means to Learn," *The STEAM Journal*, 2, no. 1 (2015). DOI: 10.5642/steam.20150201.3

11. Suzanne Choney, "Why do girls lose interest in STEM? New research has some answers - and what we can do about it," *Microsoft* https://news.microsoft.com/features/why-do-girls-lose-interest-in-stem-new-research-has-some-answers-and-what-we-can-do-about-it/ (accessed February 10, 2019).

12. "Welcome to the Hub!," *Innovation Hub*, https://innovation.fsu.edu/#about (accessed February 10, 2019).

13. More information about the Hub can be found at the Hub's website:

14. "Robert K. Godfrey Herbarium," *Robert K. Godfrey Herbarium*, http://herbarium.bio.fsu.edu/

(accessed February 10, 2019).

15.   Rita McGrath, "Management's Three Eras: A brief History," *Harvard Business Review*, https://hbr.org/2014/07/managements-three-eras-a-brief-history (accessed February 10, 2019).

BIBLIOGRAPHY

Catterall, Lisa. "A Brief History of STEM and STEAM from an Inadvertent Insider." *The STEAM Journal*. 3, no. 1 (2017). DOI: 10.5642/steam.20170301.05 (accessed February 10, 2019).

Choney, Suzanne. "Why do girls lose interest in STEM? New research has some answers - and what we can do about it." *Microsoft*. https://news.microsoft.com/features/why-do-girls-lose-interest-in-stem-new-research-has-some-answers-and-what-we-can-do-about-it/ (accessed February 10, 2019).

Lalli Hills, Adrienne, Rob Weisberg, and Catherine Devine. "MCN2018: Humanizing the Digital." *Museum Computer Network* (blog), March 6, 2018. http://mcn.edu/mcn-2018-humanizing-the-digital/ (accessed February 10, 2019).

Maeda, John. "STEM + Art = STEAM." *The STEAM Journal* 1, no. 1 (2013). DOI: 10.5642/steam.201301.34 (accessed February 10, 2019).

"MakerSPACE at Newwark Museum." *Newark Museum*. https://www.newarkmuseum.org/makerspace (accessed February 10, 2019).

"Maker Space." *New York Hall of Science*. https://nysci.org/make/maker-space/ (accessed February 10, 2019).

"Making." *Institute of Museum and Library Services*. https://www.imls.gov/issues/national-issues/making (accessed February 10, 2019).

Radiziwill, Nicole, Morgan Benton, and Cassidy Moellers. "From STEM to STEAM: Reframing What it Means to Learn." *The STEAM Journal* 2, no. 1 (2015). DOI: 10.5642/steam.20150201.3 (accessed February 10, 2019)

"Rhode Island School of Design Launches STEAM Map to Demonstrate Global Activity and Support for the Movement." *Rhode Island School of Design*. https://www.risd.edu/news/for-press/press-releases/rhode-island-school-of-design-launches-steam-map-to-demonstrate-global-activity-and-support-for-the-movement/ (accessed February 10, 2019).

"Robert K. Godfrey Herbarium." *Robert K. Godfrey Herbarium*. http://herbarium.bio.fsu.edu (accessed February 10, 2019).

"Welcome to the Hub!" *Innovation Hub*. https://innovation.fsu.edu/#about (accessed February 10, 2019).

McGrath, Rita. "Management's Three Eras: A brief History." *Harvard Business Review*. https://hbr.org/2014/07/managements-three-eras-a-brief-history (accessed February 10, 2019).

Chapter 16

We've Been Bought by the Digital Revolution

Matt Popke
Sarah Wambold

Authors' note: In November 2018, a group of approximately 25 people, including the authors, came together for a roundtable discussion called "Computer Lib/Nightmare Machine: Technology's Impact on Cultural Communities" as part of the Museum Computer Network annual conference. This essay builds on that conversation.

The pervasive network of information that we connect to every day–often times from portable devices that we carry with us every waking minute of our lives–is watching us.

We freely post moments from our days on social media, often giving very little thought to the distance that information travels, or the transfer of ownership that takes place when we hit "Share." We wear robots on our wrists to count our steps or monitor our heart rates, without thinking about the trail of habits we unwittingly expose.

We tell ourselves these tools help us to build communities or help us achieve our goals. We willingly trade our data for the promise of convenience and connection.

Museums make similar tradeoffs. Institutions invest money, time, and effort in, and consign their content to tools that promise organization, distribution, and reach. When the financial stakes are high they do their due diligence—gathering stakeholders, assessing platforms and frameworks, modeling workflows, researching peers. When the tools are free, there is less scrutiny.

In "Are We Giving Up Too Much?" Koven Smith calls for a moral and ethical reckoning of the digital systems museums use, citing the consequences of corporate values at odds with museum missions.[1] His assertion is that until recently most museums have rarely ascertained a company's ethics or paused to understand the nuanced outcomes that these complex systems trigger.

While the conversation about technological ethics may often be overlooked in the museum sector, these conversations have been going on for decades beyond our walls. When Whitfield Diffie testified before the U.S. House of Representatives regarding proposed cryptography legislation in 1993 he warned against creating a ubiquitous network of surveillance that would give the U.S. government the power to listen in on all private communications within and across its borders.

According to Diffie's testimony, "No right of private conversation was enumerated in the constitution. I don't suppose it occurred to anyone at the time that it could be prevented. Now, however, we are on the verge of a world in which electronic communication is both so good and so inexpensive that intimate business and personal relationships will flourish between parties who can at most occasionally afford the luxury of traveling to visit each other. If we do not accept the right of these people to protect the privacy of their communication, we take a long step in the direction of a world in which privacy will belong only to the rich."[2]

In 1976 Diffie, along with Martin Hellman, developed the Diffie-Hellman key exchange algorithm that secures millions of internet services today. In the 90s Diffie joined the activist movement to prevent the Clipper Chip surveillance initiative from becoming the law of the land. The idea of granting our government the power to spy on on our private lives was considered unconstitutional and a dangerous overreach.

But we live in a world now where private companies can surveil us almost as deeply as was proposed by any legislation. Every website that we connect to keeps a record, at least temporarily, of every connection. This, in itself, is not so bad. Most web servers cannot relate those connection records to individual users or to a larger pattern of behavior. But there is a growing number of servers that can.

Facebook, like other social networks, knows something about the identity of every one of its users, and Facebook records all of the activities of the users on their networks. The theory is that the more Facebook knows about your habits and behaviors, the better they can predict what kinds of advertisements you are most likely to respond favorably to, which they can then sell to companies and political organizations.

This quest to better understand their users has extended beyond the reach of their own services. In February of 2009 Facebook introduced the "Like" button. Including the like button on a web page made it possible for a Facebook user to share that page on their social feed without needing to use Facebook directly. The idea behind the Like button is to make sharing easier and increase the likelihood of web page content being shared on Facebook. But for Facebook users who have not opted out, merely loading the Like button in your web browser without interacting with it is enough to tell Facebook what pages you are looking at.[3] Moreso, Facebook tracks the behavior of users who do not have Facebook accounts on the Facebook site and also through social engagement widgets such as the like button.[4]

Facebook offered website owners a poisoned apple that was difficult to resist. Website publishers could have easy access to millions (now billions) of Facebook's users through "likes," and all it cost them was giving Facebook a record of every visit to their website. The Like button was widely adopted and then widely copied by other social networks with little thought to the potential consequences.

No one knows who will ultimately benefit from the data that is collected because the advertising can be sold to anyone: companies, political campaigns, government agencies. Should museums be comfortable participating in this vast privately owned network of surveillance? Should museums trust Facebook and other companies to use the data they collect responsibly? What have they done to earn that trust?

The End of Optimism and the Cost of Free

It's easy to single out Facebook. The last several years have seen a cascade of revelations about the company's practices that have made headlines around the world. But the problem is not limited to one company. Providing free services to users who are targeted with ads based on the surveillance of their activities has become a common business model for many of the most successful companies in the tech sector.

In an article for *New York Magazine* titled "An Apology for the Internet—From the Architects Who Built It," journalist Noah Kulwin writes: "To keep the internet free—while becoming richer, faster, than anyone in history—the technological elite needed something to attract billions of users to the ads they were selling. And that something, it turns out, was outrage. As Jaron Lanier, a pioneer in virtual reality, points out, anger is the emotion most effective at driving 'engagement'—which also makes it, in a market for attention, the most profitable one."[5]

Lanier continues, "What started out as advertising morphed into continuous behavior modification on a mass basis, with everyone under surveillance by their devices and receiving calculated stimulus to modify them."[6]

New research by Sabina Mihelj, Adrian Leguina, and John Downey looking at cultural participation and the digital divide argues that even as more communities are coming online, the gap in cultural participation is not closing. "Even if digital media become equally accessible to all socio-demographic groups, this does not mean that people from traditionally underrepresented groups will start using them to access publicly funded cultural content, even if such content is made freely available online."[7]

Their research looks at the compounding effects of the first-level digital divide (lack of access to the internet) with the second-level digital divide (skills or knowledge gaps) while acknowledging the impact of market-driven incentives at the foundations of online tools. "A large majority of search engines and recommendation systems that operate in this environment, and which shape citizens' digital cultural diets, are driven by commercial considerations rather public interests. As such, they operate on the principle of market segmentation, seeking to tailor recommendations to specific niche markets rather than aiming for universal access."[8]

Kulwin points out that the effects of market segmentation in an online context has antithetical impacts in the pursuit of creating community.

"The advertising model of the internet was different from anything that came before. Whatever you might say about broadcast advertising, it drew you into a kind of community, even if it was a community of consumers. The culture of the social-media era, by contrast, doesn't draw you anywhere. It meets you exactly where you are, with your preferences and prejudices—at least as best as an algorithm can intuit them. Microtargeting' is nothing more than a fancy term for social atomization—a business logic that promises community while promoting its opposite"[9]

A Call for Humanity

What should we, as museum technologists, do? There is value in our current "best practices." We accept that marketing and promotion are necessary tasks for our organizations. And we acknowledge that these activities need to be taken online as much as anything else. Being able to evaluate the effectiveness of those efforts helps us steer those efforts in the most effective directions.

It is difficult to tell stakeholders in non-technical departments that we want to take valuable and useful tools away from them. That task is harder when the tools are ones that we may have approved of or even advocated for in the past. But that should not stop us from reevaluating our current practices.

The first step could be one of outreach and education. We need to speak openly with our museum colleagues about the ethical issues we face as institutions in order to define a common set of values that can guide our decisions.

Executive Director of the Institute for the Future Marina Gorbis said, "We need technologists who understand history, who understand economics, who are in conversations with philosophers. We need to have this conversation because our technologists are no longer just developing apps, they're developing political and economic systems."[10]

Gorbis' call for technologists to listen to and learn from experts in the humanities is one that museums can respond to. Museums are fortunate when compared to tech startups in that they already have humanities professionals on staff. Museums are uniquely prepared to establish an open dialogue between experts that the rest of the technology sector could learn from.

Once we have defined a set of shared institutional values we, as museum technologists, can use those values to help us evaluate the tools available to us and determine their fitness to our institutional principles. When we find that the tools we are already using do not fit, we can look for alternatives. It is likely that ethical alternatives to some of our tools do not yet exist, but they never will if we do not start asking for them. We may have to make tradeoffs in the short term while we work toward a more comprehensive end goal.

We may also be surprised by the relatively low sophistication of the free, surveillance-supported tools we use. Many of us have relied on third-party tools for so long, we've never investigated what level of effort they represent. We may be pleasantly surprised to discover that much of what we use these tools for can be easily replaced.

Museums are also well positioned to include the voices of our constituent communities in this dialogue. And we should make efforts to include those members of the community whose voices have not typically been heard. The negative effects of networked technology have an outsized impact on communities of color, those with disabilities, and those with low incomes.[11]

As we expand our efforts to include these underserved communities in our programming we must take care to not contribute to systems that exploit them. The ethical concerns we face in our technology departments—of which participation in surveillance is only one—should be considered a component of the larger systemic issues that our institutions are beginning to address as we seek to become more inclusive spaces.

As institutions of public trust, museums need to take a stance on the issue of privacy and surveillance. If we don't engage with the issue now we may find ourselves talking about the concept of privacy as part of an exhibition, a cultural artifact of the distant past.

NOTES

1. Koven Smith, "Are We Giving Up Too Much?," *MUSEUM*, no. 1 (January 2019): 12-15.

2. Whitfield Diffie, "The Impact of a Secret Cryptographic Standard on Encryption, Privacy, Law Enforcement and Technology," Transcript of Testimony before Congress, May 11, 1993, https://www.epic.org/crypto/clipper/diffie_testimony.html (accessed February 10, 2019).

3. Amir Efrati, "'Like' Button Follows Web Users," *The Wall Street Journal,* May 18, 2011, https://www.wsj.com/articles/SB10001424052748704281504576329441432995616 (accessed February 10, 2019).

4. Kurt Wagner, "This is how Facebook collects data on you even if you don't have an account," *recode,* April 20, 2018, https://www.recode.net/2018/4/20/17254312/facebook-shadow-profiles-data-collection-non-users-mark-zuckerberg (accessed February 10, 2019).

5. Noah Kulwin, "An Apology for the Internet - From the Architects Who Built It," New York Magazine. April 13, 2018, http://nymag.com/intelligencer/2018/04/an-apology-for-the-internet-from-the-people-who-built-it.html (accessed February 10, 2019).

6. Ibid.

7. Sabina Miheji, Adrian Leguina, and John Downey, "Culture Is Digital: Cultural Participation, Diversity and the Digital Divide," New Media & Society, January 20, 2019, doi:10.1177/1461444818822816.

8. Ibid.

9. Noah Kulwin, "An Apology for the Internet - From the Architects Who Built It."

10. Heather Kelly, "AI Is Hurting People of Color and the Poor. Experts Want to Fix That," *CNN Money,* July 23, 2018, https://money.cnn.com/2018/07/23/technology/ai-bias-future/index.html (accessed February 10, 2019).

11. Heather Kelly. "AI Is Hurting People of Color and the Poor. Experts Want to Fix That," *CNN Money,* July 23, 2018, https://money.cnn.com/2018/07/23/technology/ai-bias-future/index.html (accessed February 10, 2019).

BIBLIOGRAPHY

Diffie, Whitfield. "The Impact of a Secret Cryptographic Standard on Encryption, Privacy, Law Enforcement and Technology." Transcript of Testimony before Congress, May 11, 1993. https://www.epic.org/crypto/clipper/diffie_testimony.html (accessed February 10, 2019).

Edes, Alyssa, and Emma Bowman. "'Automating Inequality': Algorithms In Public Services Often Fail The Most Vulnerable." *NPR*. February 19, 2018. https://www.npr.org/sections/alltechconsidered/2018/02/19/586387119/automating-inequality-algorithms-in-public-services-often-fail-the-most-vulnerab (accessed February 10, 2019).

Efrati, Amir. "'Like' Button Follows Web Users." *The Wall Street Journal*. May 18, 2011. (https://www.wsj.com/articles/SB10001424052748704281504576329441432995616 (accessed February 10, 2019).

Garun, Natt. "The selfishness of Google Duplex." *The Verge*. May 09, 2018. https://www.theverge.com/2018/5/9/17335710/google-duplex-phone-call-ai-assistant-service-industry (accessed February 10, 2019).

Gassee, Jean-Louis. "We Once Saw Technology As Liberating." *Monday Note*. April 01, 2018. https://mondaynote.com/we-once-saw-technology-as-liberating-e8b424264b1c (accessed February 10, 2019).

Kelly, Heather. "AI Is Hurting People of Color and the Poor. Experts Want to Fix That." *CNN Money*. July 23, 2018. https://money.cnn.com/2018/07/23/technology/ai-bias-future/index.html (accessed February 10, 2019).

Kulwin, Noah. "An Apology for the Internet - From the Architects Who Built It." New York Magazine. April 13, 2018. http://nymag.com/intelligencer/2018/04/an-apology-for-the-internet-from-the-people-who-built-it.html (accessed February 10, 2019).

Mihelj, Sabina, Adrian Leguina, and John Downey. "Culture Is Digital: Cultural Participation, Diversity and the Digital Divide." *New Media & Society*, January 20, 2019. doi:10.1177/1461444818822816.

Penn, Jonnie. "AI Thinks like a Corporation-and That's Worrying." The Economist. November 26, 2018. https://www.economist.com/open-future/2018/11/26/ai-thinks-like-a-corporation-and-thats-worrying (accessed February 10, 2019).

Smith, Koven. "Are We Giving Up Too Much?" *MUSEUM*, no. 1 (January 2019): 12-15.

Tippett, Krista, and Anand Giridharadas. "When the Market Is Our Only Language." *The On Being Project*. November 15, 2018. https://onbeing.org/programs/anand-giridharadas-when-the-market-is-our-only-language-nov2018/ (accessed February 10, 2019).

Wagner, Kurt. "This is how Facebook collects data on you even if you don't have an account." *recode*, April 20, 2018. https://www.recode.net/2018/4/20/17254312/facebook-shadow-profiles-data-collection-non-users-mark-zuckerberg (accessed February 10, 2019).

Wu, Tim. "The Tyranny of Convenience." *The New York Times*. February 16, 2018. https://www.nytimes.com/2018/02/16/opinion/sunday/tyranny-convenience.html (accessed February 10, 2019).

Chapter 17

Exquisite Empathy

Jason Alderman, Elizabeth Bouton, Rachel Ropeik,
Mimosa Shah, Beck Tench

*At MCN 2018, we held a workshop of empathy-building activities
and explored the following questions:*

Exquisite Empathy

 How can we uphold our human-ness amidst immense,
technological change?

 How can we use technology, if at all, to create more immersive,
embodied experiences that bring wonder and joy?

 How might we use technology, if at all, for our benefit without
harming ourselves and other individuals?

*In using these questions as our framework, we found ourselves—again and
again—expanding our conversations to look at empathy in any context, not only in
the context of technology. Often the answers that we found applied to technology
required a human-centered approach that applied beyond technology alone.*

*We put together a zine[1] to guide our workshop, and here (in reviewing how it went)
we wanted to keep the same playful, punk spirit. As we address the questions above,
we'll use a variation of the Surrealist game "exquisite corpse," taking turns with the
cursor, and Frankensteining our individual thoughts together into a patchwork.
Each author is identified by a different font, for the freedom of semi-anonymity.*

Ready? Let's begin...

---

[1] http://cloudchamber.cc/for/mcn2018/DIYempathiZINE.pdf

How can we uphold our human-ness amidst immense, technological change?

A return to <u>convivial listening</u>[2]: I recently started reading poems again, words arrayed on a screen or more preferably

scattered

on   a

page,

listening to my voice echo the words in my mind, pausing   to capture the melody or staccato of the author's voice in mine. Technology can both flatten and expand the particularities of soundtracks we inhabit. Reckoning with the unique musicality produced in our spaces is one way to (re)assert our humanity. Museums have the power to reproduce the particular while making space for each visitor to receive, inhabit, and remix the soundtracks received via their interactions with each artifact.

*(I **love** the media-analogy here: experience as mixtape[3]! Reproduce a particular experience; in the playback, allowing people to live in it, but remix it.)*

Riffing on this direction—technology as a tool for looking at our own lived experiences and culture and *human-ness*—perhaps we can also flip it on its head and make the converse true: museums can provide context (and space to talk and think about) the human history of technology, so that we can better consider how to fit technological change into our lives. If human-ness is a mixtape, the museum can look at the players we use to listen to it—phonograph, walkman, discman, iPod, *clouuuuud*—, and show how past inventions changed culture so that we can conscientiously steer our culture.

To duck away from the overly-meta metaphor: in addition to understanding each other in a technology-mediated world, understanding the historical context of how we faced immense technological change in the past can help us cut through the technology today, and museums can do that, too.

---

[2] https://onbeing.org/programs/mary-oliver-listening-to-the-world/
[3] Image by Namroud Gorguis on Unsplash: https://unsplash.com/photos/FZWivbriOXk

How can we use technology, if at all, to create more immersive, embodied experiences that bring wonder and joy?

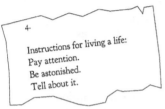

4.

Instructions for living a life:
Pay attention.
Be astonished.
Tell about it.

Attention with feeling (inspired by the examples raised by poet Mary Oliver[4]): we have the potential to be more aware, cognizant of the world we not only inhabit but also the worlds we long to be part of.

This idea of "attention with feeling" is one that guided the process of planning our Empathy Jam session at the MCN 2018 Conference. Although many of our early conversations were skeptical about technology's ability to foster these kinds of immersive, embodied experiences, we did indeed rely on key technological tools to put attention and emotion into not only our session planning, but the bonds forming between our team members. Prime among these was our insistence on Zoom videoconference meetings to do most of our significant planning face-to-face with people who lived across the span of the entire USA.

Maybe we'd have been able to make faster progress if we relied more on email, but it was when we were emailing back and forth that our conversations frequently petered out. I'm as guilty as the next person of sitting there with an un-responded-to email in my inbox, and I was sometimes the person who derailed our planning with a delayed email reply.

In our Zoom meetings, on the other hand, the creative juices flowed with all of us in our respective home and work environments, grinning and nodding and taking notes when we gathered in real time. The real-time, voice and video connections between us led to much more honest emotional investment than emails ever could.

---

[4] https://www.nytimes.com/2019/01/18/well/mary-olivers-poems-taught-me-how-to-live.html

How might we use technology, if at all, for our benefit without harming ourselves and other individuals?

Right now, technology is designed to be as functional and efficient as possible. Perhaps we can better use technology for our benefit when we design it to accommodate the messy and complicated experience of being a human using technology.

tag you're it!

One thing that became clear in the discussions in our session and in planning our session is the need to involve people from outside disciplines and different backgrounds when designing experiences—without technology and ESPECIALLY with technology. There's been a lot of discussion of ethics in the tech world[5] recently, and two techniques that seem very helpful for framing this approach, in addition to including a more diverse group in your team, are...

1. Designated Dissenter[6] — a role on your design team, rotating with each project so that one person doesn't always end up the killjoy, with the explicit duty to disagree! To question all design decisions and "asking how changes in context or assumptions might subvert those [underlying] decisions." How things might go wrong?
2. Personas Non Grata — building off the suggestion in the article above on figuring out "imperfect personas[7]," or what your audience types might be like when they're stressed or not having the best day, identify the audience types that are explicitly bad actors[8], who might abuse the experience or other participants, and design safeguards in the system to prevent that.

That's a "defensive driving" approach, though; what are ways that we can actively steer toward better ways? (We left this an open question, and maybe the act of leaving it an open question IS the way, ...to let in the right answers?)

---

[5] https://www.future-ethics.com/
[6] https://alistapart.com/article/design-for-real-life-excerpt#section8
[7] https://alistapart.com/article/design-for-real-life-excerpt#section2
[8] https://www.gaijin.com/2015/04/designing-for-evil/

(The session!)

We chose a participatory style of session to better facilitate activity-based discussion, while also adding some variety for attendees. Creating a "zine," or self-produced magazine, was a wonderful opportunity to combine the team's creativity and provide something for participants to keep.

Each team member created two unique empathy activities, referencing resources listed at the end of the zine. The session began with a centering exercise, where one participant would sit across from another. Looking into each other's eyes, <u>prompts from the speaker</u>[9] provided a personal, humanizing experience. The participants were then split into five groups, led by each team member. Each group did two ten-minute empathy activities from the zine, including a discussion. There were an additional five minutes for the groups to speak on technological implications per their activity. The session ended with a grounding exercise for participants to share what their groups discussed with the rest of the room.

Empathy is a heavy topic. Discussions get personal, and some vulnerability is necessary to connect with others. We decided to add some levity to the session as an icebreaker for participants. We advertised our early morning session through twitter and word-of-mouth with promises of doughnuts. A looping video of <u>a Sesame Street character learning the definition of empathy</u>[10] played as attendees entered the room. When splitting into groups, a game of musical chairs decided where they would end up.

---

[9] https://www.ramdass.org/wp-content/uploads/2014/12/Just-Like-Me-Meditation.docx
[10] https://www.youtube.com/watch?v=9_1RtlR4xbM

(How the session went...)

During our session I was struck by how participants reacted. Here we were, on day 3 of the conference. It seemed that those who opted to join us were there very specifically to engage. What they might not have guessed is the level of engagement we were asking for.

Our first activity, *"Just Like Me,"* illustrated the power of holding another's gaze and thinking deeply about our connection to one another, even as strangers. I saw people with tears in their eyes as they began to break out to the smaller sessions.

And in the midst of those smaller discussions, people were thoughtful in how they responded not only to the activity prompts but also each other, sharing space for feelings that they might not have anticipated.

One of the activities was about The Believing Game, to listen *completely* and *open-heartedly* to someone you disagree with and try to find ways that what they are saying might be true. When we discussed a story from the New York Times[11] about a 27-year-old evangelical from Nebraska who said

before, when you'd say you are a Christian, that would signal you are a critical, judgmental person. I feel a little bit more safe now [that Trump was elected], going into places and saying, "I'm a Christian."

...and the idea that declaring yourself a Christian was "unsafe" in the U.S.A. (in some way) *challenged* a lot of participants. Some attendees brought up later in the conference that they were still thinking about this perspective.

---

[11] https://www.nytimes.com/2018/11/01/us/young-evangelicals-politics-midterms.html

(This page unintentionally left blank.)

And then...

I'm sad to do this, and I don't exactly know the best way, but I need to bow out of our project.

Everyone else, collectively, thinks

{{{ …!!!! Things are too busy! **We should have done that, too!** }}}

Then in emails:

Thanks for letting us know. 😬

I'm so SO glad you ARE doing so ... hope that you are not feeling the stress too keenly!

—that's SO completely understandable, and to be perfectly honest, I probably should have done something similar in stepping back given the rest of what's on my plate right now.

I just want to reiterate how grateful I am for you all.

[These messages] are such gifts! They spark the realization that the human using the technology is the pivotal piece. That no matter how crass or elegant it is, the technology (be it eye glasses that allow one to focus their gaze more clearly during a "Just Like Me" meditation or the various GUIs and infrastructure that supported these very emails) is secondary to the empathetic humans connecting to each other through its use.

So.

(hammer time?)

There came a point in our collaborative writing experiment when our responsive contributions were trailing off. Life circumstances changed for several of us, and in the name of *empathetic self-realization*, we decided to take what we had written to that point and, with some small additions *(like this bit right here)*, format it to present our contribution to this book as a meta-writing exercise.

So here we are, sharing our thoughts with each other and ultimately acknowledging that our process of working on this together naturally seemed to come to a ceasing point.

When the realities of all of our lives brought other things to the fore that needed to take precedence, it only seemed right that our sense of collaboration and empathy should let us stop where it felt natural, rather than trying to force a conclusion or a shape to our writing that

Contributors

Greg Albers | Production Editor

Greg Albers is a technologist and digital literacy advocate. He is interested in the intersection of websites and books, the development of open source software and open, digital culture, and tugboats as a metaphor for museum work. He is currently the digital publications manager at the J. Paul Getty Trust, and serves on the MCN Board of Directors.

Jason Alderman | Author

Jason Alderman is an experience designer / creative technologist / jack of all trades in San Diego who consults with museums and small companies on both physical interactives and digital infrastructure projects. He gets excited! about! too many things.
Chapter 17. Exquisite Empathy

Suse Anderson | Editor

Suse Anderson, Ph.D. is Assistant Professor, Museum Studies at The George Washington University and host of *Museopunks*—the podcast for the progressive museum (presented by the American Alliance of Museums). Anderson is currently a Visiting Technologist at the Pew Center for Arts and Heritage in Philadelphia. In 2017/18, she was President of MCN (Museum Computer Network) and was Program Co-Chair for its annual conference in 2015/16. She holds a PhD and BFA from The University of Newcastle, Australia, and a BArts from Charles Sturt University, Australia.

Elizabeth Bouton | Author

Elizabeth Bouton is the Exhibits Associate at George A. Smathers Libraries, University of Florida and curator for the Albert H. Nahmad Panama Canal Gallery. She received a Master's in Museum Studies from UF concentrating in Anthropology, and continues her research of empathy in physical, online, and traveling library spaces.

Chapter 17. Exquisite Empathy

Jessica BrodeFrank | Author

Jessica BrodeFrank is the Digital Collections Access Manager at the Adler Planetarium. She holds a Master's degree in Museum Studies from George Washington University. In conjunction with her work, she is conducting research into heavy-edit metadata, digital curation and the impact digital technology can have on inclusive and diverse narratives

Chapter 9. Talking Inclusion with the 2018 MCN Scholars

Clare Brown | Author

Clare Brown is the Chief of Design for the National Museum of American History, Smithsonian Institution. Clare is a human-centered designer with degrees in Cultural Anthropology, Museology, and over 20 years experience designing exhibitions for large-scale history museums. She is currently working on a doctoral degree in the topic of "Exhibition Design as Experience Design."

Chapter 11. Slow Change

Isabella Bruno | Editor & Author

Isabella Bruno is an experience/exhibition designer at National Museum of American History, Smithsonian Institution and previously, The National September 11 Memorial & Museum. She is guided by the belief that museums offer a public service and should be designed for staff and visitor well-being in order to guarantee their perpetuity.

Chapter 11. Slow Change

Alli Burness | Author

Alli is an Executive Designer at ThinkPlace, a global consultancy applying human-centered design and systems thinking for public value. Bringing over 12 years of museum experience, she leads a portfolio of cultural sector projects, applying academic and design research, strategic communications and design expertise. She is Co-Chair of Sydney Arts Management Advisory Group, a not-for-profit organisation providing professional development tailored to arts workers, and regularly publishes and presents on the value of creative digital expression.

Chapter 7. Performing the Museum: Applying a Visitor-Centered Approach to Strategy, Experience and Interactions

Lori Byrd-McDevitt | Author

Lori Byrd-McDevitt is the Manager of Digital Content and Social Media at The Children's Museum of Indianapolis, the largest children's museum in the world. Lori holds an MA in museum studies from Indiana University-Purdue University Indianapolis. Day to day, Lori coordinates content across the museum's blog and numerous social media platforms. She is most proud of her experience managing and nurturing online communities, from Wikipedia and #musesocial to the Mommy and Daddy blogosphere. Her research centers on the concept of Open Authority, a term she developed to describe the integration of open, collaborative digital communities with museum dialogue and interpretation.

Chapter 3. Reimagining Social Influencers through an Invitation Culture

Megan DiRienzo | Author

Megan DiRienzo is an Interpretive Planner at the Detroit Institute of Arts. She developed successful interpretive engagements for major exhibitions at the Detroit Institute of Arts including *Diego Rivera and Frida Kahlo in Detroit* (2014), *Dance! American Art 1830—1960* (2015), and *Samurai: Beyond the Sword* (2013).

Chapter 6. Humanizing Augmented Reality with Lumin

Meagan Estep | Author

Meagan Estep believes deeply in the power of online tools to create conversation. An experienced educator and technologist, she crafts inventive social media strategy and content for an art museum in Washington, DC.

Chapter 5. Cultural Spaces After the Internet

Max Evjen | Author

Max Evjen work at Michigan State University (MSU) in the Department of Theatre, is core faculty in the Arts & Cultural Management and Museum Studies, and Digital Humanities programs, and is Performing and Digital Engagement Specialist at the Michigan State University Museum.

Chapter 10. Closer Than They Appear: Drawing Lessons from Development Processes for Museum Technology, Exhibitions, and Theatrical Productions

Jim Fishwick | Author

Jim is an Assistant Curator at ACMI, where he designs experiences and develops exhibitions, and other stuff about the relationship between visitors and narrative. In the theatre world, Jim specialises in interactive, intimate and immersive performance, and is the General Manager of the award-winning Jetpack Theatre Collective.

Chapter 7. Performing the Museum: Applying a Visitor-Centered Approach to Strategy, Experience and Interactions

Ariana French | Author

Ariana French is the Director of Digital Technology at the American Museum of Natural History in New York City. She leads delivery of digital products and helps create compelling strategies for technology at AMNH.

Chapter 13. AI, Visitor Experience, and Museum Operations: A Closer Look at the Possible

Amy Hetherington | Author

Amy Hetherington holds an MA and a PhD in museum studies from the University of Leicester. She has worked in the museum sector for 10 years and is currently the managing director of North American operations for Surface Impression.

Chapter 12. "Virtual Accessibility": Interpreting a Virtual Reality Art History Experience for Blind and Partially Sighted Users

Hannah Hethmon | Editor

Hannah Hethmon is a consultant and producer specializing in all things podcasting for museums and cultural nonprofits. She is the creator and host of the AAM award-winning podcast, *Museums in Strange Places*, and the author of the book *Your Museum Needs a Podcast: A Step-By-Step Guide to Podcasting on a Budget for Museums, History Organizations, and Cultural Nonprofits*. Hannah holds an MA in Viking and Medieval Norse Studies from the University of Iceland and is a Fulbright alumni.

Castle U. Kim | Author

Castle Kim is a Ph.D. student at Florida State University School of Information. Castle's study interest is in art integration into STEM experiences (STEAM). Castle has also been involved with emerging and maker technology, such as 3D printers and laser cutters, by closely working with the FSU Innovation Hub.

Chapter 15. When a Summer Camp, Innovation Hub and an Herbarium Meet: How Steam Collaboration Can Build a Humanized Experience with Technology

Andrew Mandinach | Author

Andrew Mandinach is a media producer who uses social media as a platform to facilitate conversations through emotion and wonder. Formerly of Balboa Park, Drew is the Social Content Manager for the UCLA Anderson School of Management. He credits MCN for enabling him to bridge the gap between video production and social media management.

Chapter 4. Humanizing the Video: A Reflection on MCN's Media Production Process

David McKenzie | Author

David McKenzie works as Associate Director for Interpretive Resources - broadly defined as exhibitions and digital history - at Ford's Theatre Society, a theatrical company that serves as the partner of the National Park Service at Ford's Theatre National Historic Site, particularly in creating exhibitions and museum technology.

Chapter 10. Closer Than They Appear: Drawing Lessons from Development Processes for Museum Technology, Exhibitions, and Theatrical Productions

Darren Milligan | Author

Darren Milligan is the director of the Smithsonian Learning Lab and the senior digital strategist for the Smithsonian Institution's Center for Learning and Digital Access in Washington, D.C. He specializes in user-centered and research-based development of tools and services for making online cultural and scientific heritage resources accessible and useful to educators and learners.

Chapter 14. Teachers Gonna Teach Teach Teach Teach Teach: Capturing the Now-Visible Meaning Making of Users of Digital Museum Collections

Andrea Montiel de Shuman | Author

Andrea Montiel de Shuman is a Digital Experience Designer at the Detroit Institute of Arts where she leads public-digital experiences. Andrea is involved in collaborations with AAM, MCN, Smithsonian Latino Center and Knight Foundation. She is interested in exploring how digital tools can serve traditionally underrepresented audiences, especially indigenous communities.

Chapter 6. Humanizing Augmented Reality with Lumin

Peter Pavement | Author

Peter Pavement is the director of Surface Impression, a digital design and development agency that specialises in work for the cultural sector. Peter has been working with museums and heritage organisations for over 17 years, helping them to create engaging digital interfaces and has a PhD from the University of Leicester. www.surfaceimpression.digital

Chapter 12. "Virtual Accessibility": Interpreting a Virtual Reality Art History Experience for Blind and Partially Sighted Users

Matt Popke | Author

Matt Popke is a software developer and designer at the Denver Art Museum.

Chapter 16. We've Been Bought by the Digital Revolution

Seema Rao | Editor & Author

Seema Rao is the principal for Brilliant Idea Studio. Seema has worked in museums for nearly 20 years at the interstices of visitor experience, education, and technology. She heads Brilliant Idea Studio, a firm that helps museums develop the best experiences for their visitors. Additionally, she employs her drawing and teaching skills to develop books that blend meaning-making, creativity, and visual appeal. Her third book, *Self-Care for Museum Workers*, was released in November 2017.

Chapter 7. Performing the Museum: Applying a Visitor-Centered Approach to Strategy, Experience and Interactions

Ed Rodley | Editor

Ed Rodley is an experience designer who has worked in museums for over twenty-five years. He is currently the Associate Director of Integrated Media at the Peabody Essex Museum. He manages a wide range of media projects, with an emphasis on temporary exhibitions and the reinterpretation and reinstallation of PEM's collections.

Rachel Ropeik | Editor & Author

Rachel Ropeik is a museum educator and museum adventurer currently serving as Manager of Public Engagement at the Solomon R. Guggenheim Museum. She is always in pursuit of the unexpected museum experience and wants museums to be places that inspire change and wonder.

Chapter 8. Abandon Your Recipes: Three Keys to Building Experience Sessions and Why You Should Try It

Chapter 17. Exquisite Empathy

Mimosa Shah | Author

Mimosa Shah is curious about many things, and that curiosity continues to inspire her to work in libraries and museums where informal lifelong learning is championed. She's currently the Adult Program Coordinator at Skokie Public Library, and when she's not working, she's an avid amateur photographer.

Chapter 17. Exquisite Empathy

Cathy Sigmond | Author

Cathy Sigmond is a Research Associate at RK&A, Inc., where she works with museums across the country to help them understand their audiences through strategic planning, research, and evaluation. Her approach blends traditional social science and design-based practices. Cathy is based in Washington, DC and can be reached at sigmond@rka-learnwithus.com.

Chapter 2. Calm Technology in Museums

Marty Spellerberg | Author

Marty Spellerberg is the founder of Spellerberg Projects, a contemporary art space in Lockhart, Texas. A digital media consultant, Spellerberg has worked internationally with art museums, film festivals, and artists.

Chapter 5. Cultural Spaces After the Internet

Beck Tench | Author

Beck Tench is a wife, daughter, friend, teacher, gardener, cyclist, kind stranger, and PhD student at the University of Washington Information School. She has deep and abiding curiosities about contemplative practice, technology, and public space. Specifically, she's interested in how space and technology can be designed to facilitate contemplative experience.

Chapter 17. Exquisite Empathy

Alicia Viera | Author

Alicia Viera is an Interpretive Planner at the Detroit Institute of Arts where she facilitates meaningful connections with art. She holds a Ph.D. in Art Education/Arts Administration from Florida State University. Her research interests include edu-curation, visitor-centered and multilingual exhibitions, supported interpretation, multiculturalism, and inclusivity in art museums.

Chapter 6. Humanizing Augmented Reality with Lumin

Elena Villaespesa | Author

Elena Villaespesa works as an Assistant Professor at the School of Information, Pratt Institute. Her research areas of interest include user research and evaluation, digital strategy, and data visualization in the museum sector.

Chapter 13. AI, Visitor Experience, and Museum Operations: A Closer Look at the Possible

Sarah Wambold | Author

Sarah Wambold is the director of digital media at the Clyfford Still Museum in Denver where she leads digital strategy and initiatives. Her diverse portfolio of projects includes web design and development, storytelling and video/audio production, digital publishing, and UX research. Her education includes graphic design, journalism, and arts management.

Chapter 16. We've Been Bought by the Digital Revolution

Chad Weinard | Author

Chad Weinard is a technologist and strategist for museums. His recent work explores collections, data, infrastructures, creative technology and digital cultures. Chad's background is in fine arts, art history, design, and web development. He currently leads digital initiatives at the Williams College Museum of Art.

Chapter 1. A Theme for Museum Technology

Humanizing the Museum: Unproceedings from the MCN 2018 Conference, First Edition

April 1, 2019

Published by the Ad Hoc Museum Collective

Edited by Suse Anderson, Isabella Bruno, Hannah Hethmon, Seema Rao, Ed Rodley, and Rachel Ropeik

This publication was produced using Quire™, a digital publishing platform created by Getty Publications and owned by the J. Paul Getty Trust.

Any revisions or corrections made to this publication after the first edition date will be listed here and in the project repository at https://github.com/ad-hoc-museum-collective/humanizing-the-digital, where a more detailed version history is available.

CPSIA information can be obtained
at www.ICGtesting.com
Printed in the USA
FSHW022021140419
57255FS

9 781091 360334